Ordinary Life, Extraordinary God

Ordinary Life, Extraordinary God

Dreams, Visions, and Miracles in the Everyday

LOUISE GRAY

RESOURCE *Publications* · Eugene, Oregon

ORDINARY LIFE, EXTRAORDINARY GOD
Dreams, Visions, and Miracles in the Everyday

Resource Publications
An Imprint of Wipf and Stock Publishers
199 W. 8th Ave., Suite 3
Eugene, OR 97401

www.wipfandstock.com

PAPERBACK ISBN: 978-1-6667-3630-4
HARDCOVER ISBN: 978-1-6667-9441-0
EBOOK ISBN: 978-1-6667-9442-7

04/01/22

To Jesus,
"You appeared, and the soul felt its worth."[1]

1. Placide Cappeau, *O Holy Night* (1843).

Come to *me*[1]

---

1. With these three simple words, Jesus beckons to us in over sixty scriptures in the New Testament.

Contents

Introduction

to the *Extraordinary* in the Ordinary

FROM ACROSS TIME AND space to the early twenty-first century, Christ demonstrates his love for and fidelity to us in innumerable ways. He operates through signs and wonders, miracles and revelations, amongst other extraordinary phenomena. The former, sometimes referred to by the world as coincidence, accident, or luck have occurred in my lifetime time repeatedly, and grace some of the pages of this book. Miracles open to humanity that which appears to be highly improbable and inaccessible and do not enter into the economy of what one deserves. In a miracle such as healing or deliverance, for instance, transformation takes place in living matter without changing its uniqueness, such that a person is the same except s/he is healed of and/or freed from a spiritual, physical, psychological, or other malady or from circumstances that are insurmountable.

Shadrach, Meshach, and Abednego in the Old Testament book of Daniel, are tossed into a blazing furnace, but do not even smell of smoke when they emerge from out of it. In the case of Moses, a bush burns but is not burnt. Miracles in the New Testament "dignify rather than diminish men and women because it shows that God does not appropriate or annihilate human nature in redeeming and perfecting it."[1] Additionally, miracles interrupt

---

1. Boughton is referring to the miraculous two natures of Christ here, but the description is applicable to miracles in general. Boughton, "More Than Metaphors," 315.

and "do not accept natural process," yet "preserve" the natural order in its distinction.[2] Through Christ, the natural elements and people are repaired and restored without affecting the nature of these phenomena. This is not to enter into a discussion of the truth or falsity of miracles or the miraculous, but to demonstrate how *another world* that materializes in the form of miracles as well as visions and supernatural encounters has been made manifest in my life since I was a child, and more intensely since conversion to Christianity. This is not unusual—the Bible is a living, dynamic, and effective agent, full of plans, promises, and predictions for individuals, groups, nations, and the universe that come to pass. Christian literature is another site of recorded marvels that has engaged the transcendent in the realm of immanence. Of late, the human realm teems with the marvelous, and more new media forums enable expression of the walking-talking miraculous.

Spiritual maturity wasn't my forte after Christian conversion, but God was pursued with determination and sincerity despite deficiencies and flaws. Otherwise ordinary, life at times was not very Christian and consistently challenging. Holding on to Jesus was all one could do in difficult times. Paradoxically in holding on to him, *I* let go, dialogued, pleaded, wept, and waited. Over time, even this selfish, haphazard approach bore fruit. This clinging onto him over a long period of time was rewarded. His interventions into my reality are the most enriched aspects of my life and the two years of wilderness were a spiritual feast at the same time as being the most excruciating. The oppositional war of the wilderness is best expressed by Charles Dickens in *A Tale of Two Cities*: "It was the best of times, it was the worst of times, it was the age of wisdom, it was the age of foolishness, it was the epoch of belief, it was the epoch of incredulity, it was the season of light, it was the season of darkness, it was the spring of hope, it was the winter of despair."[3] The wilderness can as such be characterized as being the vector of two existentially different and destabilizing orders: this world and *another*. One outcome from the desert experience was learning

2. Boughton, "More Than Metaphors," 315.
3. Dickens, *Tale of Two Cities*, 1.

that harvest not only refers to souls entering *another world* but also, as in 2 Cor 9:10, as provision of a harvest of generosity so that we, Christians, can be kind to others.

The focus of this book is on what God has done repeatedly for someone, namely myself, who has been quite indistinguishable in other respects. He does the same outside of myself as my many examples will corroborate, despite potential refutation from some philosophical quarters. The capacity of God to do absolutely anything at any time for anyone without blowing his own trumpet, both masks and marks the power and extent of his love to improve human circumstances. His work in the world is visible when we humble ourselves and open our eyes and ears to *his world* in our own. His intimate knowledge and care for the human, animal, and plant world is unmistakeable despite hype on the outward appearance of things. As God quizzes Job, "Who gives intuition to the heart and instinct to the mind"? (Job 38:36).[4] "Who provides food for the raven when their young cry out"? (Ps 50:10). "I know every bird on the mountain" (Job 38:41). "Do you know when the wild goats give birth"? Have you watched as deer are born in the wild"? (Job 39:1). Wild animals have appeared to me to be all alone as they are born, live and die. Not so says the God who converses with Job!

Incredibly, "God watches how people live; he sees everything they (we) do" (Job 34:21). While it is difficult to accept what happened to Job, we also know that he was a precursor to the suffering servant Jesus, and from them we receive an understanding of God as committed to life, of humans, animals, and birds as well as the elements required to sustain life, such as the rain, rivers, vegetation, and so on. Ultimately, Job humbly understands and responds, "I know that you can do anything, and no one can stop you" (Job 42:1). My experience has been similar in this respect: as a slow and assured process of realisation through encounter with God the Father, Son, and Spirit who bring *another world* into my own. His omniscience is posed rhetorically in Ps 94:9, "Is he deaf—the one who made your ears? Is he blind—the one who formed your eyes?

---

4. Unless otherwise indicated, all Scripture quotations are taken from the New Living Translation.

He also knows what we are thinking (Matt 9:4; 12:25; Ps 94:11) and what we are going to say before it becomes audible (Ps 139:4).

Messiah Jesus in the New Testament enacts this ability to do anything: defying the laws of physics by manipulating the natural elements by opening the religious cage from which God was mistreated, misunderstood, and locked in; producing limbs from stumps, emancipating people from evil, and transforming one thing into another: sweat into blood into wine; an enemy of Christians into apostle of Christ extraordinaire, and providing unlimited access to God the Father, Son, and Spirit. Jesus manifests the activation of a new kind of *love* in word and real time indiscriminately, single-handedly overturning the history of human evil while inviting the not yet human and all too human other into the open embrace of his Father's love[5] through his life in this world; a feat that ultimately necessitates complete self-displacement-effacement-renascence. One vision recalled on page 74, captures such a moment of giving of self, of love, without being seen, it can be shown, is the extravagance of a prodigious, unrecognized, love. God doesn't need human permission to be himself: to give wastefully and to love unreservedly.

The following acknowledgement of what God has done in my life is inspired by the Psalmist of Ps 105:1 who encourages the believer to "proclaim his (God's) greatness and let the whole world know what he has done" and, "tell everyone about his wonderful deeds." Like many others, I am a living witness to the bounty of a God who is alive and ever-present in the universe and infinitely available to all. Anything other than perfect love is foreign to God the Father, Son, and Spirit—that's why his mercies to us are renewed every morning, and he reciprocates ugly misdeeds and thoughts with his goodness in the form of forgiveness and the grace with which we overcome.

While brief narratives express and form the everydayness of the extraordinary, love, the problem of evil in the world, Christ, Christianity, and the Christianized West are also considered.

---

5. 1 John 4:8, 16: "God is love" discloses the ontology of God as love.

Introduction

The supernatural experiences that follow are not in chronological order, but are nevertheless contextualized to facilitate meaning.

1

Is Anything Too Difficult for the Lord[1] in the Here and Now?

IT IS STRATEGIC THAT this chronicle of God's entrances into my reality begin in the middle of a storm, a real deluge on a cold, Melbourne morning. God does all things well, including downpours of the real and metaphorical variety. What is most appreciated about storms is this: I meet the real God, not the one shackled by human moorings to interpretation, analysis, extrapolation, and/or denominational theology. The latter has its place in exploring the nature of the *extraordinary*, but these events are actual instants of God's intervention in the warp and woof of the everyday, displacing and denuding constructions of himself[2] while exceeding all expectations. These visits enrich and are sharper than any two-edged sword because they are the Word enacting itself in deed. This gives credibility to an idea of God by Aquinas, who once wrote, "God is pure

1. Jer 32:27 and Gen 18:14. Unless otherwise indicated, all Scripture quotations are taken from the Holy Bible, New Living Translation, copyright © 1996, 2004, 2015 by Tyndale House Foundation. Used by permission of Tyndale House Publishers, Carol Stream, Illinois 60188. All rights reserved.

2. The pronoun "him" will be used out of convention.

actuality."[3] What's more, in all his grandeur he appears to the most ordinary, not just the giants of the faith, indicating his commitment of inextricability from the world of humans, plants, and animals.

Melbournians were experiencing a torrential downpour after a long period of very little rain. This was the first day of a new semester, and the first tutorial I would facilitate. The car is parked a half hour's walk away from the university, off campus, for the simple reason that parking is free. After parking, there was no option other than to sit in the car wondering how to get to the university dry without an umbrella. This outpouring was completely unexpected and prompted prayer that the shower would stop just long enough for me to get to the campus center. Once there, an umbrella could be purchased.

Imaginings of a bedraggled woman entering her debut tutorial rained trepidation while the noise of the storm on the outside competed for my full attention. Initial nerviness was doubled at the thought of a ruined reputation.

Pinned inside the car, the violent storm blurred the outside of every window and produced a fine mist on the inside. Finally, after about ten minutes, expecting to be completely soaked, and late to boot, after grabbing my bag, I opened the car door. The unabashed rain stopped instantly and completely, downright. Astonished and jolted, the long walk to the campus center began, completely dry. On the way, one tiny, icy raindrop landed directly on the middle of my head, causing me to look up and remember the finely refined and attuned power of God. He had been waiting for me to get out of the car; I waited for him to stop the rain before getting out of the car. He was more patient; it required of me the faith sufficient to only open the car door. Was it faith or necessity? The latter, in all honesty, which had the effect of driving home the importance of faith. He did the rest, modeling a metaphor that would persist for the next twenty years of my future. The rain started again about one hour after reaching my destination, totally dry.

Spiritual storms, intermixed with drought, sowed and farmed the seeds of my wavering faith. As Hosea realized, God "shall come

3. Lacugna, *God for Us*, 151.

unto us as the rain, as the latter and former rain unto the earth"
(6:3). That is, as one interpretation has it, after the sowing and the
harvest of the word. Echoing Jesus in John 17:3, on the importance
of knowing God, Hosea 6:3 continues, "Let us know; let us press
on to know the Lord; his going out is sure as the dawn; he will
come to us as the showers, as the spring rains that water the earth."

He received nothing in return for that feat of the miraculous;
it was not beamed on social media, but instead, a change crept
into my mind and heart of seismic nature in which a Scripture was
corroborating itself through this experience: ask anything of the
Father in my name, Jesus pleads, and he will do it (John 14:13, 14;
16:23).

On the Thursday before Good Friday a few years later, while
facilitating a tutorial, the ability to teach suddenly vanished, leaving me struggling to get through a three-hour session. Late that
afternoon, exhaustion had the upper hand on the way home via a
forty-five-minute drive, while realizing quite quickly God had or-
chestrated this incident for good effect. For the first time teaching
was seen as a gift, a blessing, and generous thanks accompanied
an apology as a kind request was made to restore the ability. It
was, after the Easter break. Yet, it was also self-evident as it was
to Job that, "God gives and takes away." This Scripture is, as my
experience proved, followed by "Blessed be the name of the Lord"
(Job 1:21).

On this same drive home, confusion had set in on reflecting
on a conundrum: some people in church prayed to the Father, others to the Father and/or Son and still others were moved to call on
the Holy Spirit, or a combination of the above. Very few prayed to
the Father, Son, and Spirit because these three are one, and talking with one, usually to me, includes the other. Yet the question
persisted since at that time, everything was taken to Jesus.

Working in two places, doing a lot at the church and a family
of four delightful but needy males had taken a toll on my energy
levels, such that, on opening the front door after returning home;
my husband said something to me which was brushed off. *Just let
me relax please*, I thought. Persistent, he stood at the door of the

room annoyingly and as my bag was put away, he quite loudly asserted in a booming voice, Jesus says, "all authority in heaven and on earth has been given unto him" (Matt 28:18). Then he repeated it. Yes, the answer to my question was prompt and comforting; fortunately, God doesn't give up, particularly when we are not in synchrony with his generosity or too tired to care.

At about this time something very frightening occurred. My son James, then fourteen, confided in me that he was experiencing auditory hallucinations which had two dominant effects. They terrified him to the point where he requested I sleep on the floor of his room at night in order to reassure him. As well, he tended to spend quite a lot of time outside doing physical activity because as a result, the hallucinations were rendered less compelling to him.

Although it was a busy time at work, every spare minute was spent trawling through the medical databases at the university for information that could offer insight into his condition. Whilst the condition may have been caused by an illness picked up while travelling through some countries in Africa with his father previously, it is also clear that young people a few years older than him commonly experience the first symptoms of schizophrenia. I needed to act fast. Taking him to a psychiatrist was a very real possibility, but it could take years to address his condition. Prayer took over. I had already learned to pray in the gaps while teaching. A very tricky request was sent to Jesus, based on all the remarkable feats he had accomplished in my life up to that point. Husband Geoff furnished prayer cover for supply of sufficient faith, which was milked for all it was worth. The hallucinations stopped abruptly, releasing James into complete recovery and freedom from fear within a week of relentless, intense prayer. God has proven time and again that he is able to accomplish more than we may ask or imagine (Eph 3:20), uprooting mountains by the power generated by a grain of faith in him; a skerrick is sufficient for all purposes. Faith is the guarantee of what one requests, but it too is a gift from God[4] and available on request. The Bible was living, breathing, and acting in my life, one Scripture and sometimes more, at the same time. Challenges

4. Rom 4:16.

are unavoidable in life, Christian or not, and can be truly frightening, but God's response to them is to defy the laws of the natural order in rescuing us from them, which has the effect of deepening our trust in his existence, extraordinary intervention, and defence beyond process.[5] The KJV of Ps 4:1 already declared this pearl of wisdom three thousand years ago: "thou has enlarged me when I was in distress."

5. 1 Cor 10:13.

2

The Bible's Bias and Cogency of God Communicating through Dreams, Visions, and Other Supernatural Means

Every book of the Bible witnesses to God communicating in ways other than the ordinary. Dipping in and out of each with brevity will serve to establish this parallel universe of supernatural communication. Spiritual inundation of the anthropological order in the New Testament is followed through to present day witness in literature and new media.

In Gen 28:10–15, "as Jacob slept, he *dreamed* of a stairway from the earth up to heaven and the angels of God were ascending and descending on it." He *sees* God and also *hears* him say, "I am the Lord, the God of your father Abraham and the God of Isaac," who *prophesises* to Jacob, "I will give you and your descendants the land on which you are lying. Your descendants will be like the dust of the earth, and you will spread out to the west and to the east, to the north and to the south." Jacob is told he and his family will be blessed and God will accompany and oversee his affairs throughout his lifetime. Continuing to usher the future into the present, "I will bring you back to this land. I will not leave you until I have done what I have promised you."

Some other examples in Exodus include God appearing to Abimelek in a dream one night and telling him to return Sarah to her husband Abraham (Gen 20:3). Laban is also visited via a dream (Gen 31:24). "Genesis 20:3, 28:12–15, 31:10–13, 24 are auditory dreams and Genesis 37:5–10, 40:5 and 41:1 are symbolic and require an interpreter."[1] Genesis 15:1 (ESV) records a *vision*: "After these things the word of the Lord came to Abram *in a vision*, saying, 'Do not fear, Abram, I am a shield to you; Your reward shall be very great.'" Examples in Genesis are multifarious and cannot all be presented here.

In Exod 3:15, Moses hears God ask him to remove his sandals, marking the beginning of an extraordinary long-term relationship between the two, that travels between the devil and the deep red sea. "Fire blazed forth from the Lord and consumed the burnt offering" when the glory of God materialized to the whole community in Lev 9:24. Aaron's rod buds, blossoms, and fruited ripe almonds in the tabernacle, in Num 17:8. We learn that Moses was the humblest man on the face of the earth in Num 12:3, while Deut 1:3 has "Moses address the people with everything the Lord had commanded him to say." Joshua 6 records the disintegration of Jericho through supernatural means, and in Josh 10:12–14, God responds to Joshua's request by making the sun stand still despite the movement of time, until his battle is won. In Judg 6:36–40, Gideon's request for a supernatural sign through a fleece is granted twice. Ruth documents the godly way Boaz redeemed the land of Naomi and embraced Ruth herself.

Audibly, God calls Samuel in 1 Sam 3:2–10, and in 2 Sam 7, God talks to the Prophet Nathan in a dream about a message for King David. On and on it goes. First and Second Kings testify to the mighty works of God through Elijah the prophet, through whom the environment is controlled by drought and rain, ravens provide food in a desert place, oil is multiplied, a dead child is resurrected,

---

1. Lien-Yueh Wei, "Dreams."

food is multiplied, and after many other miracles, Elijah is whisked off to heaven in a chariot of fire by a heavenly chauffeur dispatched to carry him directly to heaven, efficiently bypassing death. In 1 Chronicles, David exclaims that God uses him to "burst through his enemies like a raging flood" and they named that place "the Lord who bursts through." Second Chronicles 11 inscribes the Lord speaking to Shemaiah to carry a message.

God "stirs the heart" of Cyrus of Persia in the very first verse of Ezra and through the "memoirs of Nehemiah," we follow his distress, repentance, prayer, and fasting before the king miraculously permits him to return to his beloved Jerusalem to re-build its walls.

God's explanation of who he is to Job is unforgettable, poignant, and astoundingly extraordinary. *Listen to his questions to Job*: "Have you ever made daylight spread to the ends of the earth, to bring an end to the night's wickedness? . . . the light disturbs the wicked and stops the arm that is raised in violence" (Job 38:13, 15). "Do you know the laws of the universe? Can you use them to regulate the earth?" (Job 38:33). "Who gives intuition to the heart and instinct to the mind?" (Job 38:36). Job 39 draws a detailed picture of the intimate knowledge and understanding of animal and bird life. Included is the powerful Behemoth, and the spiritual dragon Leviathan is referred to as having a heart as hard as rock but, is subject to God (Job 41:24).

Continuing the rhetorical vein, is this a God who is inarticulate and indifferent? From the inception of the first broken contract between God and humanity, he has endeavored to communicate with, and take an intimate interest in the anthropological order, such that, it is fair to admit as Job does, "We talk about things (in reference to God's nature and engagement with the human world) we know nothing about, things far too wonderful for me (us)" (Job 42:2). Saint Paul almost quotes Job in Rom 11:33–35 (NIV) in reiterating the acuity of the treasury of the wisdom and knowledge of God! How ungraspable his judgments, and his ways beyond tracing out! "Who has known the mind of the Lord? Or who has been his counselor? Who has ever given to God, that God should repay them?"

Remarkable in their spiritual insight, Pss 2:7, 22, and 110, written between the ninth and fifteenth centuries BC, several thousand years before Advent, prophesy about the identity of the coming Messiah. The two Testaments agree when Heb 5:5 cites Ps 2:7 verbatim, "You are my son, today I have begotten you," and Psalm 22 begins at the end of the beginning of the New Testament with, "My God, My God, why have you abandoned me," also found in Matt 27:46 and Mark 15:34. Jesus' reference to the Father interchangeably as either Father or God, beautifully frames his humanity and divinity. Psalm 22:11–22 (ESV) exposes the collision of, and competition between, spiritual and human worlds within Jesus as he terminates:

> 11 Be not far from me,
> for trouble is near,
> and there is none to help.
> 12 Many bulls encompass me;
> strong bulls of Bashan surround me;
> 13 they open wide their mouths at me,
> like a ravening and roaring lion.

The "bulls" referred to here are demons jostling for the kill of their prey: God.

The following prophesy pictures Jesus' I/self "being poured out like water," quickly and completely turned out, such that, he is "absolutely exposed, absolutely abandoned," "there is literally no shelter possible."[2] Communicated by his heart "like wax, melted within his breast" (Ps 22:14). Searing heat melts wax, signifying he has already stepped into the inferno.

> 14 I am poured out like water,
> and all my bones are out of joint;
> my heart is like wax;
> it is melted within my breast;
> 15 my strength is dried up like a potsherd,
> and my tongue sticks to my jaws;
> you lay me in the dust of death.

---

2. Agamben, *Coming Community*, 39. The citation is applied in a different context.

16 For dogs encompass me;
a company of evildoers encircles me;
they have pierced my hands and feet—
17 I can count all my bones—
they stare and gloat over me;
18 they divide my garments among them,
and for my clothing they cast lots.
19 But you, O Lord, do not be far off!
O you my help, come quickly to my aid!
20 Deliver my soul from the sword,
my precious life from the power of the dog!
21 Save me from the mouth of the lion!
You have rescued me from the horns of the wild oxen!
22 I will tell of your name to my brothers;
in the midst of the congregation I will praise you.

Isaiah 53:5 refers to the effect of this descent into hell as a crushing:

But he was pierced for our transgressions,
he was crushed for our iniquities;

Psalm 22:15 describes an omnipotent God whose strength is as dry and brittle as an ancient shard of pottery, and verse 17 prophetically photographs an emaciated Jesus so expended that "all his bones can be counted," since they protrude from his skin. Down he goes from verse 16 into a gradual descent of self into liminality, a process which produces suffering, uncertainty, "*transition, and potentiality*," according to Victor Turner and Hannah Ward.[3] The former defines "liminal *personae*" as "threshold people," because "they are between the positions assigned and arrayed by law, custom, convention, and ceremonial. . . . Thus liminality is frequently likened to death, to being in the womb, to invisibility, to darkness, to bisexuality, to the wilderness and to an eclipse of the sun."[4] Succinctly, Turner refers to this deconstruction of self and spirit as 'sacred poverty.'

3. Ward, "Boundary Dwellers," 105.
4. Turner, *Ritual Process*, 95.

Like the angels who roll the stone away in (Mark 24:2; Luke 16:4), Ps 110 (ESV) prophetically raises Jesus into an *otherworldly* status:

> The Lord says to my Lord:
> "Sit at my right hand,
> until I make your enemies your footstool."
> 2 The Lord sends forth from Zion
> your mighty scepter.
> Rule in the midst of your enemies!
> 3 Your people will offer themselves freely
> on the day of your power,
> in holy garments;
> from the womb of the morning,
> the dew of your youth will be yours.
> 4 The Lord has sworn
> and will not change his mind,
> "You are a priest forever
> after the order of Melchizedek."

The notion of wisdom is miraculous in the book of proverbs and Ecclesiastes, whilst the messianic prophecies in Isaiah predict the government of Jesus the Messiah and peace will never end, and is repeated in the same verse: "He will rule with fairness and justice . . . for all eternity" (Isa 9:7). Through Isaiah we hear God say this: "only I can tell you the future before it even happens" (Isa 46:10).

Jeremiah was prophetically trained from an early age when the almighty instructs him, "Look, I have put my words in your mouth" (1:9). As Jeremiah's spiritual sight is shaped and sharpened, he is asked repeatedly, "What do you see?" as spiritual visions appear before him that he is trained to read with blistering, spiritual insight.

The anguish of God's seeming lack of supernatural activity is the general tenor of Lamentations. The book of Ezekiel commences with his visions of God, and Daniel is well-known as having visions of end times, surviving lions, and receiving a visitation from the angel Gabriel, among other noteworthy spiritual turns and twists. Hosea played God when his personal life mirrored the infidelity of the human relationship with God, from God's perspective. Joel too is a carrier of God's messages to his people as was Amos. The book of Obadiah is a vision, and Jonah was swallowed by a whale when he refused to respond accordingly to God's request to save the Ninevites. Micah had visions (Mic 1:16), Nahum had visions concerning Nineveh (Nah 1–3) and Habakkuk is replete with visions. Prophetic utterance and insight are given to Zephaniah and Haggai, Zechariah, and Malachi.

A long silence of many hundred years precedes the Gospels of Mathew, Mark, and Luke which open with a rich outbreak of dreams and visions and miracles before the birth, during gestation and after the birth of Christ as angels appear to Zechariah, to Mary prior to conception, and prior to that, the conception of John the Baptist to elderly parents. Joseph has dreams that direct his wife and son out of Bethlehem and again later, back to Nazareth. Overall, the New Testament is so crammed with the supernatural that one can only infer heaven has well and truly come to earth, and Jesus was no ordinary baby. Such supernatural activity doesn't attend every birth despite every birth being special!

The word "fulfilled" occurs several times early in Matthew's Gospel, as the prophecies about the messiah given in times past materialize. This activity is extended and heightened as Jesus increasingly displays abilities never seen before as well as extending and redefining what it means to be human, and the love of the Father as prodigious and open to the nobody and anybody. He embodies the human as both social and *sacred* and therefore as in a process of limitless transformation and possibility. This is for example evident in his indifference to the social marks and markings that differentiate one body from another, that mark up some bodies, and mark down others on the market of ethical worth. His love for the blind, the lame, the fool, the mad, and the immoral betrays a unique capacity to stand against evil and, in so doing, attract it. As Graham Ward notes, "this man can walk on water. This man can sweat blood . . . can bring life . . . can multiply material so that 5000 are fed from a few loaves and fish. This man can heal by touch . . . [and] create wine from water."[5] In effect, Jesus

5. Ward, "Bodies," 164.

materializes and authenticates *a possible world* by what he says, is, does, and becomes in all the books of the New Testament.

Clearly differentiating him from all others, is his response to those around him. His intense affection "does not cease even when there is clearly impending betrayal and failure, when nine out of ten lepers fail to return to give thanks, when it is thrown away or forgotten. No attempt is made to distinguish between real and spurious need."[6] Gene Outka suggests further that "love's presence is somehow not determined by the other's actions; it is independent both in its genesis (he need not know who I am) and continuation (he may remain my enemy)."[7]

Out of nothing and as emergent, creation is itself set in revision, ungrounded through the supernatural abilities of Jesus' life. He increasingly reclaims the world as beloved, and his spiritual-physical body as the nexus between material and spiritual orders.

As is predicted in the suffering servant prophesied by Isa 53, Jesus is battered by the love of the father in himself that he recognises as his own truth. Jon Sobrino names the complexity of the supernatural in the event of the crucifixion in suggesting, "if God really is present in the cross of Jesus, then he is there first and foremost as someone contradicting the world and all that we consider to be good and true. God appears *specie contrarii*. It is not at all self-evident that there can be life in death, power in impotence, and presence in abandonment."[8] In the grand scheme of God's life with us through Jesus and beyond to this day, his *world* irrevocably marches firmly into this one with, and also without, humanity.

In the 1950s, Brother Richard Wurmbrand was imprisoned in Romania for close to fifteen years because his religious beliefs and activity were considered subversive to the communist regime at that time. To pass time in his interminable lockdown in a tiny cell, Wurmbrand would construct sermons in his head and preach them into his empty vault. Across the world in Canada another prisoner in solitary confinement who self-admittedly had "gone

6. Outka, *Agape*, 21.

7. Outka, *Agape*, 11.

8. Sobrino, *Christology*, 199.

astray," requested in prayer if there was anyone else like him, could the man's thoughts be conveyed to him. After Wurmbrand's release many years later, a Canadian remembered every evening "hearing sermons from far away." In a book shop one day he came across a copy of Wurmbrand's *Sermons in Solitary Confinement*. He recognized the sermons and got in touch with Wurmbrand to tell him he was not preaching to an empty cell. Wurmbrand's sermons in Romania were supernaturally broadcast to a prison cell in Canada[9] in a similar way to Elisha in Israel hearing the king of Aram in his bedroom plotting to attack Israel from another geographical area (2 Kgs 6:8–12).

George Mueller's simple prayers of faith were answered by extraordinary generosity of people he did not know or contact. Orphanages filled with street children were purchased and sustained by donations as his autobiography reveals.[10]

Brother Andrew in *God's Smuggler* would carry Bibles to Eastern Block countries during the cold war. On being stopped at check points, he would pray the Bibles in his boot would become invisible. The Bibles were never discovered despite numerous searches throughout his many trips, and that old car he used for years, survived by the grace of God. When he no longer needed that car, it completely fell apart.[11]

Rendering objects invisible through prayer also occurs in the movie version of Corrie Ten Boon's *The Hiding Place*. When she enters a Nazi concentration camp, she smuggles in a Bible despite all prisoners being stripsearched.[12]

More recently in 2002 in the publication of Brother Yun's *The Heavenly Man*, the most extraordinary feats are disclosed— miracles akin to the event of Phillip meeting and sharing Christ with the Ethiopian eunuch and baptizing him in a nearby stream, "When they came up out of the water, the Spirit of *the Lord suddenly took Philip away*, and *the eunuch did not see him again*, but

9. Wurmbrand, *From Torture to Triumph*, 40–41.

10. Mueller, *Autobiography of George Mueller*.

11. Brother Andrew, *God's Smuggler*, 113.

12. Collier, *Hiding Place*.

went on his way rejoicing. Philip, however, *appeared at Azotus* and travelled about, preaching the gospel in all the towns until he reached Caesarea" (Acts 8:26–40 NIV). Time travel no less, or what sci-fi refers to as teleportation, otherwise referred to by the Bible as the power of the Holy Spirit. Likewise, John 6:21 has Jesus walking briskly on a rough sea to join his fearful disciples on their boat during a storm; as soon as Jesus steps on their boat they were *instantly transported to the shore.* Emulating the Heb 1:10–12 description of time and space being folded like a blanket.

Brother Yun writes of how during the "strongest revival in China, miracles were so commonplace" that "they were as natural as breathing the air."[13] They brought countless people to faith and strengthened the faith of others.

An anonymous peanut farmer goes to sleep one night and has a dream. He is told he will govern the country of his birth. He becomes governor despite competition and then President of the United States. Generally referred to as a man with peace coursing through his veins and persevering with building homes for the poor since his presidency, among other exceptional achievements, Jimmy Carter's Christian faith is remarkable. From him I learned that forgiveness is an art and "a way of life."[14]

The only difference between biblical times and contemporary times is the polymorphic and poly-directional existence of the supernatural. Note the number of converts from Islam to Christianity, who in their testimonies have had dreams and visions that have led to their belief and faith in Christ.[15] For information of how Messiah is drawing secular and orthodox Jews to himself, visit *One for Israel*, and listen to some of the unusual testimonies. Watch how this organization of young Jewish Christians on one of the most intransigent front lines, ploughing the rockiest of soils, is defending the faith with determination, indescribable courage, and spiritual beauty of word and deed.

13. Brother Yun, *Living Water*, 153.
14. Carter, *Sources of Strength*, 68, and 22.
15. Any search engine will provide a harvest.

For an experience of exceptional Nabi and Seer prophets in action, Sam Robertson and Sara-Jane Biggart respectively, visit *GPC Power Hour* on YouTube. As in the manifestation of the prophesies of old, Joel 2:28–32 and Acts 2:17 guarantee in the last days heaven will flood earth in the form of miracles given to ordinary people to, I believe, enable us to "contend earnestly for the faith once and for all that God entrusted to us (Jude 1:3). Hebrews 2:3–4 reiterates, "signs, wonders and various miracles, and gifts of the Holy Spirit are distributed according to his [the Father's] will," as authentication and imprimatur of the salvation to a *life in God* embodied and awarded by his son Jesus.

3

The Reward to Those
Who Suspend Doubt[1]

A Home of Unusual Supply
Despite Financial Hardship

DOCTORAL RESEARCH WAS ACCOMPANIED by financial struggle chiefly because of raising a young child independently since divorce from his father when he was aged two. The rental property lived in was to be sold and a new rental was required with very little money. Unfortunately, a place could not be found in time. Moving in with family was the only option. The drive each morning was over an hour, only it was very pleasant as my son James was a raconteur, never short of enthusiasm or words. Shameful and soulful encapsulated the view of myself as a parent. No one wants to be in tight, alienating situations. George Steiner's description of Abraham in his dilemma is applicable to anyone in a spiritually demanding situation: "no synagogue, no *ecclesia* can house Abraham as he strides in mute torment, towards his appointment with the everlasting."[2] It can be inferred, therefore, that in the moment

1. Heb 11:6.

2. The appointment is the sacrifice of his son. Steiner, "Wound of

of crisis no one else can take my place, such that, the "individual," whether it be Abraham or someone completely ordinary, is irreplaceable and indispensable to their circumstances, hence recourse to the always present empath: Jesus.

In the moment of acquiescence, de Caussade describes what it means to subsist in and depend on God: "when the soul has discovered this divine influence it leaves all its good works, its practices of devotion, its methods of prayer, its books, its ideas and consultations with spiritual people in order to be under the guidance of God alone by abandoning itself to this influence which becomes the one and only principle of its perfection."[3] In trusting God, one feels foreign, alone, and vulnerable yet inextricably assimilated to life in the everyday. Navigating extremes, temporal exigencies through spiritual enigma, violently includes the absolutely excluded *other*: God's will in this life. "God unsettles the sojourner by forever calling him (her in this instance) from a secure present to an insecure and uncertain future";[4] such is the experience of faith as Saint Paul describes it in Eph 4:22–24 and Rom 8:36.

Late afternoon, we would trek back through fading light, looking forward to dinner and grateful to have a place to stay despite the circumstances.

Living conditions were physically comfortable, except for the lack of light in the dark space, and prevention of opening a blind to even listen to the sound of a blackbird in early Spring, joined forces with a general feeling of segregation by distance. Two weeks after arriving, it had become clear we would have to move, finances aside. One morning surrounded by darkness in a room that appeared underground, James and I held hands and my words tumbled out and in front of us like a contortionist: Could we have a place to live, not far from James' school and within my widow's mite? Even though the desire for a view was not articulated, within me *vistas broke into bright light and blinds were pulled up on the*

Negativity," 108.

   3. De Caussade, *Self-Abandonment*, 83.

   4. Taylor, *Journeys to Selfhood*, 260.

current place and also previous place, both shaded and cramped, inhibiting our vitamin D intake. That darling little face in front of me lit up full of faith like a firefly in the night!

On a grey, wet Saturday morning, the search began for rental properties in the *Melbourne Age* newspaper. At that time, many people had not made the complete move to electronic information for things like rentals. The classifieds were devoid of rentals in the areas we should move to. Silently I said to the creator of the universe even before setting off, *I am going out and will not return until we have a place.* With James still asleep in his bunk and family willing to mind him, I set out suffering immense anxiety.

Towards late afternoon, a few rentals visited made my heart sink. My mind shifted back to a Christmas when James, at four, reveled in the one present placed in front of him when I wanted to lay the world at his feet, wings at his heel, and fantastic, delicious, epicurean morsels on a table of virgin marble in a tropical garden with jolly minstrels, hanging Jacaranda and toucans. Toucans were his favorite bird. Peals of childish delight sent a dozen toucan frocked in soft purple Jacaranda into flight and sent me back to the astronomical rents in Northcote. Refusing to give up and with disabling anxiety, the newspaper was scanned again. There was one line describing a flat that was obscured by the other adverts which contained so much detail. Not only that, the rent was what the Spirit had prepared me for. After picking up the key from the real estate office, the small block of flats was not only located on the same street as the place we had rented before, but on occasions during my morning run/walk, I would look up and covet that unreachable upstairs flat. This was precisely the flat that was vacant. I walked in and was certain we would live there. It was clean, safe, and had impossible views, and was also fairly close to, in being a short tram ride away from, James' school.

On submitting an application, only to be told that the real estate agent had made an error with the rent. The flat was apparently more expensive than had been advertised, however, even though real estate agents in Melbourne never ever make such a concession, this agent, Nelson Alexander, did honor the error and allowed rental at the advertised sum. That flat was the epitome of blessing for years. Secure and protected, prayer life budded wings and soared in the way the mountains did in the horizon from our living room balcony. The blinds were indeed lifted to reveal views of immeasurable pleasure at all times of the day in gobsmacking artistry and generosity of the sandaled one. The Kandinskys, Jeff Walls, and Pro Harts paled into the colors, expanse, light, and cloud formations on a continuous basis throughout the day and evening at no cost and was incomparable to anything seen in a frame, and open to all. Three thousand years or so ago, the Psalmist noted the same phenomenon:

> The heavens declare the glory of God;
> the skies proclaim the work of his hands.
> 2 Day after day they pour forth speech;
> night after night they reveal knowledge.
> 3 They have no speech, they use no words;
> no sound is heard from them.
> 4 Yet their voice goes out into all the earth,
> their words to the ends of the world. (Ps 19:1–4 NIV)

Tremendous anxiety and other symptoms experienced were a form of post-traumatic stress disorder from two previous ordeals which were exacerbated with the decision to move. Family was reluctant to provide much needed practical help. Most hurtful was an accusation of being a "bad mother" in front of my son at the time. It confirmed my own worst suspicions about my parenting ability and jettisoned me back to the vulnerability of a bygone day. James, then aged nine, disagreed wholeheartedly and told me they were wrong. He was convincing, and I experienced several times how God ministered to me through him.

That flat was often closer to heaven than earth. A large tree outside our bedrooms housed birds galore who broadcast each day an orchestral cacophony of delightful affirmations of prayer. In the nascent spring of our life at that time, we recuperated gradually from three harrowing experiences that occurred one after the other in a short space of time, under the unseen hand of altruism *per se* in the hospital of heaven in Mitchell Street, Northcote.

In quiet prayer time one morning, still poor as research progressed slowly, the thought crossed my mind of using the tithe to buy James a pair of shoes. We were living on a shoestring, and he desperately needed new shoes. On the couch, looking far off into an unknown distance, a call for new shoes was sent out. On finishing, the security doorbell rang. Perhaps it was a neighbor but, the person who stood at the door was a courier who had a package. In it was a pair of heavenly, pale blue sneakers. Apparently, the previous day sister Sue had been at a shoe sale in a sports store and selected these shoes thinking James would like them. She used the courier from work to deliver them the next morning. I sat down and wept gratitude and incredulity. It came to me that even before I called, God had answered and before I spoke, he heard (Isa 65:24–25). It is also evidence that God hears the needy (Ps 69:33). There is more!

When nine years old, James' favorite toy disappeared whilst he visited his dad's house. Inconsolable as a result of living in two homes, he found comfort in this toy that he stuffed into his trouser pocket. Nightly together we agreed wholeheartedly that God would bring Squirt back somehow. Many of his prayers were answered in the most spectacular ways, except for Squirt. Some of these prayers will follow in due time. He was reassured by explaining that God had to work through people. Wooing them, God would wait till they consented, and that could take time for Squirt's return.

Discordant feet were heard slapping the hot summer bitumen hard and fast as they ran down the street two years later. A loud banging on the door followed. James was so excited he had run all the way from the tram stop that was ten-minutes away. At the door, unable to speak, he simply held out the hand that grasped Squirt. We stood in that moment looking at each other mutually hypnotized by wonder. There had been a garage sale at school, and in one of the boxes lay Squirt with his deformed tail exactly as he had been two years prior. Squirt will return in cameo later.

On another occasion, in prayer whilst sitting on the couch late morning, recollection of prayers unanswered generated sadness and loneliness. Perhaps they were not heard; even worse, is *he* saying "No"? Having fallen asleep, I was roused to discover three figures in white, very close to my left, who were looking at me, and they were heard talking about me without me understanding what was said. Why was my hypothalamus so slow? As cognizance increased, they gently disappeared and the room filled with an amazing *weight*, so much so that open-mouthed, that couch held me for an hour, unable to move, heavily suffused by the afterglow left by them. We were not alone, and deeply cared for. This God was extracting the precious from what I considered worthless,[5] myself, as he made himself known as parent, friend, and provider of aesthetic, material, psychological, and spiritual supply.

"For Brothers" is the persistent prayer that rose from James. Still single, and self-doubting, it was one of those unusual requests that was left entirely in the hands of God. Characteristically the latter responded: James' father married again and had a son, and a few years later I was married to a man with two sons, both a few years older than James.

Another persistent prayer of James' was for loyal, special friends. Over the next fifteen months a gradual and steady stream of friends emerged, like the balletic Aurora Australis, and to this day, James' call for friends has been honored, including his supportive, motley, matchless, Christian friends from St Hil's in Kew, each worth their weight in gold, frankincense, and myrrh.

Despite suffering what may have been PTSD, ultimately, anxiety and fear were overruled, for as Rom 5:21 bequeaths, as believers, we are under the rule of *grace*. God had become my staunchest ally. James claims that life in that flat with me was the happiest part of his childhood. The preacher and prophet Emma Stark is correct when she says, the most spectacular view of God and what he can do comes after the hardest seasons.[6]

5. Jer 15:19.

6. Based on a variation on a hiking quote by an unknown author.

4

Joy for Mourning[1]
When Death Is Expected

A FEW YEARS AFTER conversion and foundational in impact, this narrative will backtrack to an existential firestorm. At seventeen months, after being sickly since about eleven months, James became very ill. Together then, his father and I were living in a very pleasant country town about six hours from Sydney. On the day signs of illness emerged, he was in Melbourne at a conference and since we had only lived in that town a short time, I lacked the confidence to ask his acquaintances for support. When he telephoned that evening, he was informed anxiously that James was unwell, and perhaps should be taken to hospital, which was only a five-minute drive away. Cautiously, he dissuaded me. Instead, later that evening on my own initiative a physician was called who did not diagnose anything, increasing my instinctive uneasiness.

Panadol was administered every four hours to very little effect. James' fever was very high. He was submerged in a bath often to bring his temperature down. Having fallen asleep close to him around three o'clock in the morning despite being concerned, a gentle breeze almost like a wing brushed against my cheek very

1. Isa 61:3.

lightly. It was 5:00 a.m. Instantly, the presence of an angel was sensed with a very gentle voice within persistently prompting me to take him to the hospital. On call to the hospital and during the conversation, tears intruded, and the nurse told me to bring him in if I was worried. James was put in a pale green hand-knitted cardigan even though he was very hot.

Outside, a nondescript morning presented unlike the morning of his birth when my feet sank into the muddy path left by a storm. Through the rear vision mirror, he looked grey, but reminiscent of a bird, a joyful red robin or sparrow perhaps, creatures that have been a source of joy to me since days of old. The little bundle rarely murmured or cried, even whilst ill.

On arrival, the medical staff was alarmed as he was injected, x-rayed, and wired to machines, as well as attached to IV. He had pneumonia. After he was stabilized, I was told that had he not been brought in when he was, perhaps he would not have survived. We were in the hospital for four days. Returning home to have a quick shower a day or two after initial admittance at hospital, a noticeable strip of hair on the left side of my head had turned white. It was reminiscent of a book titled *Germinal*, by Émil Zola, in which the protagonist Étienne Lantier goes completely white-haired after a traumatic experience when an underground mine caves in.[2] Love had entered my world and it was being seriously threatened.

Less than a month later, he became critically ill once again. Sadly, it also became evident at this time that the relationship between his parents was broken. Once again, it was pneumonia and one of the physicians suspected and speculated that he may have cystic fibrosis and would not survive past his fifteenth birthday. This was said to me, not his father. This time the hospital injected him with a "new wonder drug" and told us to take him home. It was the night of December 22, a Sunday. Church had not been attended since arriving in this town for reason that it was too difficult with a young child who was unwell often. But on this night, the Uniting Church service provided a warm, wooden bench in the last row. The female minister talked about how difficult it

2. Zola, *Germinal*, 245.

would have been for Mary especially, because she may have suspected that she would lose her child at some point in the future. It resounded; loss of my child had entered my thoughts. Silently and alone, very alone, with a heart full of raw grief, the strength to continue arrived haltingly. Previous attempts to contact this minister about baptizing James had not been possible; she had been busy. Perhaps sensing my distress, she approached. My first request was, would she be willing to baptize my child as soon as possible? She made a time for 11:00 a.m. the next day, December 23. The hospital made it clear I could not fly home to Melbourne to be with my family at Christmas because both James' lungs were striated.

Late on the 22nd of December, sister Sue in Melbourne was woken up and felt compelled to make the eighteen-hour drive up to see us. She put her seven-year-old into the car, picked up father, and together they drove the eighteen hours with only toilet breaks. She arrived late on the twenty-third.

The next morning: December 23, James was to be x-rayed again to discover six patches on one lung and four on the other. At 11 a.m., my father, sister, her young son, my husband, James and I attended the church where James was to be baptized. A photo was taken by my sister. In it, the minister is holding on to James as she baptizes him, in precisely the same way Christ has his hands in the stained-glass window above their heads. It appears as if Jesus himself is carrying my son as he is baptized.

After the baptism, and for reasons still unknown, the hospital allowed us to fly to Melbourne. After dropping us at the airport, father and Sue took the very long drive back. On Christmas day James was ill again, this time, I distinctly heard the Spirit tell me that it would be the last time in hospital. It wasn't clear what that meant, but somehow one continues. The drive into the children's hospital in central Melbourne was on my own. Unfortunately, on the flight back, the airline had lost our entire luggage, including his many x-rays. Previously, his father had observed correctly, "James could light up the dark" as a result of the many x-rays, eliciting an idea of him as a Christmas tree with rainbow lights. Given his condition, James was x-rayed again in Melbourne. There wasn't a single patch on his lungs. In fact, the radiographer, and later the doctor, noted that his lungs were "pristine." Instead, he had perhaps picked up an urinary tract infection due to all the antibiotics he had been on. A majestic, rich Christmas present! Twenty-four hours after his baptism the manifest signs of healing were revealed by the x-rays. These are still in my possession.

So overwhelmingly sensational was the cure, that there was no reason to ask God why he allowed it to happen. The other gift received coming out of this storm is he had gently placed in me an unshakeable "quietness and trust in his strength" (Isa 30:15), for it was going to be required, necessary in fact, over the coming years.

James continued to improve in health while marriage to his dad collapsed, and not long after Christmas we moved back to Melbourne. Fifteen years later when James was seventeen, by car we made the long journey back to that university town. As we approached, I took a long, sideways, thirsty look at the strapping lad who was asleep in the passenger seat next to me, triggering the jubilance of David after he had taken down that foul mouthed, marauding Philistine. A "basket case" then, now, God wasn't simply words on a page of my Bible; he was in the car, on the road, as familiar as home, authentically heroic, and wildly valued. Through the months of walking on hot coals, spurred on like David with his slingshot of obedience all those years ago, Jesus had modeled how he was the doer of his own word in our lives (Jas 1:22).

After leaving that town fifteen years prior, accommodation was found in a very sleepy suburb of Melbourne, full of retirees who were wonderful neighbors. The most challenging problem was often being cash strapped. The intention was to take up full-time teaching again; until then, a master's degree required completion and we survived on very little. On one trip to the local supermarket, many groceries were required with only $25 in my wallet; frugality was called for only to be interrupted when God said to me, *get everything you need*, with me replying *okay, but I do not want to be humiliated at the checkout*. Throwing caution to the wind, everything needed made up an almost full trolley which was put though the checkout and being told that all that stuff was $24.

James received an icy pop with the dollar that remained. It was such a resounding and bewildering multiplication of the value of the Australian dollar and food in supermarket trolleys.

Quietly these marvels were pondered and noted like treasure on my computer in order to be reminded of the goodness of God in the land of the living (Ps 27:13). There was no doubt *another world* had entered my own; one that Isa 55:1 prophesied seven hundred years before the birth of Jesus and enacted by Jesus in John 7:37 in the feeding of the multitude: "Come, all you who are thirsty, come to the waters; and you who have no money, come, buy and eat! Come, buy wine and milk without money and without cost."

A prophetic dream that came later represented divorce as a train derailment. James emerged in front of me from the wreckage missing his body from under his arms. My body had been sliced in two, from the waist down, as I stumbled to rescue my son. So it was in reality, we were emotionally disabled for many years. James is now twenty-nine and still endures some of the consequences. Yet, only "God digs wells of joy with the spade of sorrow," as an anonymous wiseacre once said.

5

Jesus Visits, Twice
Before Indubitable Difficulties, to Presage Victory Over Them

LATER, THE NORTHERN SUBURBS of Melbourne became home because of my teaching position. We had extraordinary experiences in that house before our lives were devastated by three events that will not be recounted here and was referred to earlier.

James now refuses to talk about his experiences of Christ from that time; I will relate what he told me as I recall it. He was about four years old. He had two different experiences, both in the back garden where he spent much of his time. We were sitting in the living room reading a book on the creation story and on the page was an impression of God with wooly long white hair and a beard. He exclaimed with some authority, "God doesn't look like that!"

"How does he look?" I asked.

He replied, "God is young, has dark hair and he was wearing an old, long, brown dress. He didn't have any shoes on, but he did have large cherries on his feet. And he walked on the air."

The large cherries on Jesus' feet were a mystery for ages until the realization that the wounds on Jesus' feet have healed and looked like cherries to a young child who had no idea about the nature of his death. Apparently, Jesus came over the fence in the air and stood next to and engaged James in conversation about his two favorite toys: Squirt and Diddle. This was a few years before Squirt disappeared.

In the other experience, all James said was, "his feet were shining so brightly that I was too scared to look further."

Suddenly, I am stood in front of Jesus' towering presence, feeling two years old. There is an unequivocal sense of belonging and definite conviction that he was the only place I would ever belong. Next, I am up in the air, in the arms of possibly an angel, but instantly there is a realization it is Christ. Shining through me, there is nothing but his light in front of us as I sit in his arms facing the open with my back resting on his breast. The inclination to turn my head and look at his face was compelling, but there was great fear it would grieve and sadden me irrevocably, preventing such a turn. His strength is what was most apparent. This feeling of his invincibility is matched by, oxymoronically, his extreme gentleness and protection. Next, monumental mountains of ocean had risen in front of us, with the first being the highest. As we approached, the seven mountains, one after the other, collapsed into a calm, gentle ocean and there is only sunshine in front of us. This experience remained the balm of sanity and victory through great trials and struggles over the next ten years and beyond. In real time, those mountains of misery collapsed into the sea as in Ps 97:5: "The mountains melt like wax in the presence of the Lord."

Although alone and dealing with some shattering events, the 'Father of the Fatherless and protector of widows is God in his holy habitation' (Ps 68:5–6 NIV).

It is extraordinary that God stands beside us like a beggar in the street, humble in his efforts to get to know us so that we can access all that he is. As such, learning to stand together, I in him and vice versa, was the object, because he knows how difficult it is for his children when they shift allegiance to him as is borne out in John 16:33 and my dream; in this world challenges and dares are inevitable, but Jesus is unbeatable!

6

The Problem of Evil Resolved

Taking advantage of a blossoming faith, one revelation a day was requested. He replied with "great and unsearchable things I did not know" (Jer 33:3 NIV), that were recorded in my "decomposition book." Here is the first sample: the Old Testament is bloody and violent because people were lawless. Love is the victim there. The Hebrews who were constrained and held accountable by the Mosaic law constantly violated the terms of their very existence. So it was with other sacral and secular laws in the world that provided a moral compass with penalties for infringement. Obedience to the laws was difficult for some, impossible for others.

This revelation was actualized in 2013 on a visit to a country where the laws familiar to me did not hold and the laws that made cohabitation possible were increasingly disregarded. Every car on the road was dented and many road rules ignored. There were three lanes of cars on a two-lane road for instance. One afternoon the sight of a squillion soldiers sitting on the meridian in front of me signaled anything could happen and no one would know. Trembling like a mouse before a trap, instinct swiveled my face and body to the right towards the direction of the one church that remained in that area, which was my destination. The fact is many of the soldiers were young and probably equally fearful of what they may be called on to do. On the way there, I had passed a couple sitting, waiting for transport, when the tram lines had been filled with gravel where the solders sat just further up from them.

That experience was matched by ignorantly and unintentionally entering a men's-only carriage on a train packed to the rafters. My body could not be protected. My husband stood nearby. What of the people living in slippery states of chaos? An elderly woman hit by a car lay on the road for close to an hour in searing temperature. As soon as the police arrived the perpetrator was allowed to move on without hesitation. Finally, a chemist, a slight, young woman, held the injured woman and walked her to her pharmacy.

The question arises, when the laws themselves are inhumane and/or violated, what then? Galatians 3:19 reveals correctly that wrongdoing is exposed by the Hebraic law; we wouldn't know certain actions were unlawful otherwise, adultery being one. The law in accordance with Galatians is our guardian and provides protection and direction, acting as a deterrent to wrongdoing because it provides an inventory of what is unjustifiable and injurious to an individual and community. Law detects and identifies, but cannot repair the propensity to, or consequences of wrongdoing, unlike *grace*. Societies and communities devise their own rules and laws for protection and longevity. The erosion of these results in a lack of liberty in those subjected to them, which instinctively produces tension and concern. Galatians 4:4 is way ahead of the law in revealing that our freedom from enslavement to the law is by way of grace. "Love your neighbor as yourself" summarizes the Hebraic law with a love that includes one's lawless and inhumane neighbors through a baptism of heavenly grace within.

Like a town crier, Nietzsche's madman howls the secularization of Western culture: God is dead, or rather, *"we have killed him—you and I. All of us are his murderers. But how did we do this? How did we drink up the sea? . . . Are we not plunging continually? . . . Are we not straying as through an infinite nothing? . . . God is dead, God remains dead and we have killed him."*[1] That said, the God of

1. Nietzsche, *Gay Science*, 181.

philosophy is then strung up between quotation marks, alienated by italics, and crossed out only to be reincarnated as an afterthought parenthetically, or replaced by an obscure origin (*Khôra*), and so on, in efforts to think of God as outside(r), or *think outside God*. A significant question and revelation from this theoretical flirtation with the demise of God is, why was the death of God required—why was a covenant required to be sealed with God's blood?

"Without shedding blood there is no remission"[2] or cancellation of a penalty that comes from breaching a spiritual contract. The blood of animals was a stop-gap measure, a temporary pardon. To this day, contracts between two or more people are ratified by the law, the terms therein binding, with penalties applied for violation of them. The spiritual order is precisely the same because the Hebraic law and animal sacrifice was God-given.

The first contract between God and humanity was a tacit request as covenant, free of coercion, that humanity was at liberty to refuse. Hosea 6:7 records God saying to Israel and Judah, "like Adam, you broke my covenant and betrayed my trust," even though all that was his was given out to humanity,[3] with one request: stay away from engagement with evil.[4] The contract was broken, yet even after the betrayal, God tries to prevent evil, initially and notably as an example through saving Cain who kills his brother for following God's ways. It is the first murder recorded in the bible. The Bible illuminates a chronological and tragic trajectory between the first tacit contract through to the Hebraic law, during which lawlessness and faith are locked in a mighty enduring battle for supremacy. Between the Hebraic law and the new contract/covenant, with a refusal clause included, good and evil continue to coexist in humans. However, the latter agreement was sealed by the blood of God and is referred to as the perfect sacrifice in Heb 9:14, providing irreparable final reinstatement of that initial contract between God's way and humanity. God becomes the universal human on our behalf to fulfill that initial primordial turning

2. Heb 9:22.

3. Gen 1:28–31.

4. Gen 3:4.

away from his love, and his love of humanity. Through Jesus' faith exercised through love, God's way, that original tacit contract denotes a returning to God, given out without measure and condition. In spiritual terms there is no karma for Christ's followers (Col 2:14), but we are still subjected to the Hebraic-Christian laws of the land that make life with others more secure. Throughout, God has defied evil at the cost of his love being victimized.

Many of us, including prophets from the Bible have asked why a loving Being puts up with evil? Does God permit evil? No, but those he loves most, his human children do, and he has done and continues to do everything to convince them otherwise. It is humanity who are vulnerable to evil and akin to any loving parent, God continues to support his child/ren who have turned away from his love, and his eternal call to love. Evil is not exterminated because it would necessitate eliminating the entire human race who he calls his beloved.

That a God who is love puts up with evil in his children is best illustrated as "You have heard that it was said, 'Love your neighbor and hate your enemy.' But I tell you, love your enemies and pray for those who persecute you, that you may be children of your Father in heaven. He causes his sun to rise on the evil and the good and sends rain on the righteous and the unrighteous" (Matt 5:43–48). This reverberates in Luke 6:27–31 as

> But to you who are listening I say: love your enemies, do good to those who hate you, bless those who curse you, pray for those who mistreat you. If someone slaps you on one cheek, turn to them the other also. If someone takes your coat, do not withhold your shirt from them. Give to everyone who asks you, and if anyone takes what belongs to you, do not demand it back. Do to others as you would have them do to you.

God doesn't permit evil, he stands against, endures and dies for his enemies (Eph 3:16). On our behalf, for us and also through us, God's indefatigable love is the great counterfoil to the world's errant tendencies.

A spiritual clash continues to be evident in all Christians, including myself, many years after conversion as the human world and its desires can be difficult to refuse at times even while sanctification continues.

7

The Most Powerful Force in Heaven and on Earth[1]

On starting research in 2000, initially inane naivety and un-reasonable enthusiasm joined forces in marching determinedly towards understanding the conundrum of the Trinity. First John 4:8, 16, "God is love," provided the inexorable reason for the mul-tiplication of the One into three transferred exponentially into us post Christ: *infinite love* unperverted. A poem by Saint John of the Cross made a difference in understanding how the Trinity is unique and multiple and infinitely extendable. In real love, it is possible to be differentiated[2] without at the same time being di-vided or separated. The final stanzas from Saint John of the Cross (1542–91), "Upon the Gospel 'In the Beginning was the Word' relating to the most Holy Trinity," articulate the idea of Trinitarian love as impossible to contain. Love can step beyond the confines of one; yet the one can contain an unlimited love. This love is both

1. 1 Cor 13:13.

2. Differentiation signifies *connection* and disconnection between differ-ences held by love, and is based on a central idea in Deleuze, *Difference and Repetition*.

lover and beloved and is referred to as the "Being" of each one and of all three, that unifies while differenciating.[3]

Saint John underscores the importance of difference as essential to Christian love; without diversity, love would not be love as it holds, unifies, and amplifies the difference of each one. In suggesting the beloved is also simultaneously the lover, love is of one character and quality in Father, Son, and Spirit. Love makes these three one, without effacing, sublating, or reducing, but instead exposing the beloved in his or her difference. Saint John's poetic verse is substantiated by John 4:8, 16, "God is love itself: *Ipsum Amore.*"[4] The nature of Triune love suggests and demands a notion of *God* as infinitely open in love, to include humanity in all our splendid uniqueness and transgression whilst the *transcendent* remains *uncontaminated* by us; that is, uncorruptible, even while imbricated with the immanent, best demonstrated by the two-in-one natures of Christ. The resurrection of Christ's human nature and body wasn't factored in by the madman in Nietzsche. God does not remain dead nor do we. Instead, God as love *opens* in humanity through a new covenant forged in flesh and blood, heart and mind. Humanity, therefore, can be conceived as *within-love* not only because we have the potentiality to accommodate unsighted spiritual treasure, but this treasure manifests by virtue of the matter present. As Kierkegaard writes, "The Spirit of Holiness lives in an unclean human vessel amidst lies, arrogance and deception," such that as Madsen alludes, "the violence of the universe was at every point congruent with its nurturance."[5]

Trinitarian Love can extend and multiply in any direction while sustaining distinction that generates accord: uniqueness in community. Jean Hyppolite outlines the potential of love to *connect* without appropriative union, when he comments: "Love is the miracle through which two become one without, however,

---

3. St. John of the Cross, *Poems of St. John*, 49–51.

4. Lacugna, *God for Us*, 303.

5. Madsen formulates this idea as a question. Her argument is skewed to reflect God as the antithesis of love. As such, the original context of this citation is subverted. Madsen, "Notes on God's Violence," 235.

completely suppressing the duality. Love goes beyond the catego-
ries of objectivity and makes the essence of life actually real by
preserving difference within union."[6]

God as absolute *love*, by its very nature, enters into paradox:[7]
disturbingly in this world while remaining uncontaminated by it.
This phenomenon can be mapped through Jesus' be-attitude of
extension and expansion of himself through time and space in-
definitely. One that transgresses death by stepping into an *other*
life whilst both his feet are firmly planted in the heat and dust of
his middle-Easter world. When love takes place, not merely at the
conceptual level and/or in written form, but when it is authenti-
cated through lived experience in the world of hostility, his love
refuses violence by stepping into its place. Christ inaugurates and
reclaims what he claimed was the origin—love—in and through
matter. This *place*: his spiritual-physical lived existence can be
conceived as love because of its donation without condition across
space and time.

In Genesis, creation is permitted the act of naming which
resulted in being grounded in oppositional hierarchy. [8] Jesus, in
contrast, appears to initiate renaissance from within oppositions
by claiming them as his beloved. Out of nothing and as emergent,
creation is itself set in revision, ungrounded through this opening
he introduces in and through love of an*other* kind. Substantiating
Luke 6:32–36, love is not expended to be returned.

The *modus operendi* of the symbolic human order is to ascribe
difference in humans in an arbitrary manner, in contrast to the
movement of Christic donation which effects transmutation from
within normal life process, proceeding automatically without bias,
such that *other*worldly love is seared into the very nature of the
symbolic. His enterprise redefines the ethos of world standards,
attitudes, and conscience. That he operates from, with, and within
"a series of demands, taboos, sanctions, injunctions, prohibitions,

6. In Taylor, *Deconstructing Theology*, 9.

7. The field of metaphysics in philosophy, side by side with the proofs in
the Bible.

8. These ideas deviate from Ward, "Transcorporeality," 239–40.

impossible idealizations, and threats," obscures, and at the same time renders permanent, the profundity of *love's* effects.[9] The prolonged outward trajectory of Christic donation fulfils the law without undermining the forms and figures that are subject to its demands. To ask *who* Christ is, is to follow his indefinite movement of empowerment-disempowerment through the *sacred* towards the fulfilment of love.

In *God without Being*, Jean-Luc Marion captures Jesus' expendability of himself when he writes of love: "Love does not pretend to comprehend, since it does not mean at all to take; the giver strictly coincides with the gift, without any restriction, reservation or mastery. Thus love gives itself only in abandoning itself, ceaselessly transgressing the limits of its own gift, so as to be transplanted outside itself."[10]

Effect, outcome, and expression of love, of loving, and/or being loved is what is important because love fractures the subject: "I return broken: I come back to myself, or I come out of it [love] broken," aptly observed by the philosopher Jean-Luc Nancy, as Jesus and many humans have experienced.[11] John the Baptist[12] was to point out another facet of love demonstrated by Jesus, to increase materialization of the Father necessitated progressive donation and implantation of himself out, which in turn attracted the nobody, angered the religious somebody, and welcomed everybody.

In the context of Jer 30–31, love is the foundation, resource, and architect who reshapes and resurrects a people, the Messiah, the redeemed, and the church. Expressed differently, love makes every effort to revive, restore, and recharge the anthropological order. Henry Nouwen articulates the personal significance of living in a human world charged with the redemption of God's reckless love when he writes:

> I have the immense joy of being a *man*, a member of a
> race in which God himself became incarnate. As if the

9. The symbolic order as described by Butler, *Bodies that Matter*, 106.

10. Marion, *God Without Being*, 48.

11. Nancy, "Shattered Love," 261.

12. "He must increase, I must decrease" (John 3:30).

sorrows and stupidities of the human condition could overwhelm me, now I realize what we all are. And if only everybody could realize this! But it cannot be explained. There is no way of telling people that they are all walking around shining like the sun.[13]

This is a spiritual truth not evident to many. A thought also present in a verse from Elizabeth Barrett Browning: of the world brimming with the holy, and every shrub ablaze with God, but only those with spiritual sight remove their sandals.[14]

Kierkegaard summarizes love in 1 Cor 13 as

> the very ground of everything, exists before everything, and remains when everything else is abolished . . . but that which in the sense of perfection . . . is the greatest must also be able to undertake the business of the lesser ones [he is referring to faith and hope] . . . and make them more perfect. . . . Power, talents, knowledge, and such are . . . qualities for oneself. . . . Love . . . is a characteristic by which or in virtue of which you exist for others. [15]

Knowledge is the art of weighing, measuring, and contrasting information in a detached manner. In love distinction evaporates and even though "knowledge puffs up . . . the communication of knowledge can also be edifying; but if they are, it is because love is present."[16]

God's love is not evident because it works through the ordinary processes of life. The Old Testament book of Hosea conveys *how* a barely visible and unknowable love of God operates in time: "I took them up in my arms; but they did not know that I healed them. I led them with cords of compassion, with the bands of love, and I became to them as one who eases the yoke on their jaws, and I bent down to them and fed them."[17] Here, love gets down on

---

13. Nouwen, *Genesee Diary*, 87.

14. Browning, *Aurora Leigh*, l. 823.

15. Kierkegaard, *Works of Love*, 213, 211.

16. Kierkegaard, *Works of Love*, 204.

17. Hos 11:3–4.

his knees to support the beloved. Basic needs, liberation from that which exacts,[18] guidance, and restoration as is suggested by "healing," are said to be supplied by the love, compassion, and faithfulness of God's love even though this is not discernible. The victim at the foundation of the world and the casualty and victor of Calvary was/is a prolonged love that fiercely shields its human enemy.

The intentional humility of the *One* who is *love* enters into and cares about the small details of our lives. Deep frustration convinced me I was the wrong person to do research on love for I knew nothing about it. This was the precise reason, was the Spirit's immediate response. And it took many more years to understand through him that there is nothing I can do for him, and plenty with and through him. We were on speaking terms and appreciation expanded as a result of the way he communicated his love for me and all others around me.

For two years before commencing research, an insatiable desire to extend my learning culminated in an application that inexplicably "fell through the cracks." The consummation of prayer on this subject occurred on October 26, 1999. James had been feeling poorly and I had fallen asleep in his bed whilst tending him. We lived in Alphington at the time. On October 26, tiny stars cascaded in front of me as I sat up abruptly, perhaps a result of having hit my head. Immediately time stopped—I don't know how else to describe it. God said: "*Louise, return to your first love*," and at the same time, God presented which department and university to call. Two ideas formed simultaneously, which is not possible with time which moves chronologically. That department was called as soon as recovery made it possible. The academic spoken to couldn't promise anything, but he encouraged an application. Next, every door opened in the department referred to; it was later that this thesis almost seemed like slow suffocation by superior minds. By the way, I had forgotten October 26 was my birthday, but *he* hadn't.

Despite poring over it endlessly, "return to my first love" did not make sense. Was fine art, literature, politics, or philosophy my love? Months later in the passionate uncertainty of topic in initial

18. This is suggested by the reference to "easing the yoke."

research, a discovery was made: the return was a Scripture in the book of Revelation, and it was regrettably sad to realize that one returns only because one has abandoned one's great love.

During the seven years of part-time research, we moved home many times, anxiety was constant and chronic, my PhD supervisor got a job in a US university, and my ex-husband was demanding James spend more time with him. As poverty and ostracism seesawed out of my control, dreams, visions, and encounters became common.

Trial after trial over eleven years stripped some unjustified pride from and moved me just a little closer to an understanding of the selfless one. At these times, as Martin Buber was to reveal, "God speaks to man in the things and beings that he sends him in life; man answers through his action in relation to just these things and beings."[19] One was a woman named Rose, whose son Declan had been friends with my James since prep. The other was a beautiful charismatic Catholic woman named Jaye who constantly appeared mysteriously whenever my desperation for prayer set in. Whenever the call for reprieve went heavenward, Rose would invite James to their home. She even took him with her family on holidays. Rose and Jaye responded to God's urgings. Our adult children keep in contact.

As for Jaye, who was otherworldly and carrying a huge cross of sadness, as we stood, with Jaye holding onto her pushbike, and talked on the center meridian outside the Catholic Theological Library in East Melbourne one very hot summer's day, a *revelation* of certainty she and I would be together in heaven occurred to me. When she heard it, the largest, most joyful, toothy smile broke across her face. That same smile was beamed at me as she skipped in and out of sleep on the penultimate day of her life, a few years after that revelation.

The church attended religiously during that time was middle-class and unable to empathize with my mounting problems. Largely unsupported in a practical sense, the people on prayer duty would pray with heart, but my difficulties were kept to myself

19. Buber, *Way of Response*, 71.

for fear of being judged "needy." The truth is, like many other Christians, I *was* needy and and felt that I was spiritually inferior to others in the church. Two consequences followed: the first was a realization of not turning away when someone needed help, which is biblically supported by the narrative of the good Samaritan and also God himself hemorrhaging in body and spirit all along the Via Dolorosa in Jerusalem. Of equal importance is to trust that God has allowed experiences of all kinds as a way of maturing us in the faith and improving the world we live in, such that his ways take precedence.

Philosopher Georgio Agamben reveals a tendency among us to "oppress those who show us their weakness, and failing our innermost possibility . . . we fall away from the only thing that makes love possible."[20] Carlo Corretto, who joined the Little Brothers of Jesus and lived as a monk in the Sahara desert during the 1950s, recounts an experience in *Letters from the Desert* that illustrates this retreating in the presence of need and the indelible mark left on him by it.[21] Very early in his service to desert dwellers, while in the desert at night as the temperature plunged, Corretto had two blankets which he used to shield himself from the cold. Not long after bedding down, another man arrived who had no shelter from the cold and shivered all night. Corretto failed to share one of his blankets with that man and was besieged by lifelong remorse.

On a blazing street in Colombo where the sun was as merciless as Correto's desert during the day, I was bought an icy pop, a very rare and appreciated treat. Immediately, a child beggar younger than my myself approached and followed me closer than arms-length. I suspected what she was after: whatever remained on the stick, but once finished with, it was thrown on the ground and stomped on. Covered in dirt and debris she picked it up and licked it. Horror had borrowed me. The look on her face and her desperation to taste that icy treat could not be excised from memory. These examples bring to the fore widespread complicity in retarded notions of what constitutes human need, and how those

20. Agamben, *Coming Community*, 32.
21. Corretto, *Letters*, 3–5.

who are extremely vulnerable and dependent on our empathy, test the boundaries of these definitions in voiceless though spiritually articulate ways. God had painfully given voice to "the needy" in the above examples even though neither spoke.

Indeed, Jesus' full-time ministry was attending to the needy and one particular example is sufficient to verify his constancy to this purpose to bring justice and rescue the weak from the exploitative clutches of the skewed. In Matt 20:29–33, he is being followed by a "large crowd," in true superstar mode, when he stops, listens, and ministers to two blind men who call out very loudly to him. The fruit of the spirit are in full activation despite protestations from the crowd, when he says to the blind as he says to us today, "what do you want me to do for you"? This is not a metaphysical, figurative, or logical question. It is literal. Just as his touch gave them instant sight then, in the same way he responds to each one today. Jesus is never too busy and no one is too needy for him, as was prophesied about him in 732 BC: "a bruised reed he will not break and a smouldering wick he will not snuff out. In faithfulness he will bring forth justice" (Isa 42:3 NIV). This prophesy is cited in Matthew as an injunction that he would continue to attend to the needy until justice reaches its full potential (Matt 12:20). That mountainous sermon that begins in Matt 5:1 predicted the weakest, most destitute members of the church, society, and nations will inherit the earth and live in abundance of peace and prosperity.[22] Inheriting the earth means that all aspects of one's life will be blessed and a blessing to others. Descriptively nuanced in Ps 72:12–14 (NASB),

> For he will save the needy when he cries for help,
> The afflicted also, and him who has no helper.
> 13 He will have compassion on the poor and needy,
> And he will save the lives of the needy.
> 14 He will rescue their life from oppression and violence,
> And their blood will be precious in his sight.

---

22. Matt 5:5; Ps 37:11.

He is revealed as taking the full force of injustice into himself in Isa 53, as he increasingly became the dumping ground for vice, rejection, violence, punishment, pain, and alienation. As a deformed and pulverized spectacle (Isa 53:5), the world looked on, away from, and despised him for carrying our "neediness."

His self-abdication into powerlessness was to allow all others their potential and possibility of becoming children of God the Father, who is love. In being reduced to a locus of abuse throughout his life, and particularly at the apex of the horror of his dying, he becomes one with the universal nobody, battling alone against the forces that generate evil. In the belly of radical diminishment, he becomes the place of "irrevocable hospitality"[23] because his response of taking the path of most resistance and fulfilling his "innermost possibility of not-being" reveals the ineffable profundity of God's *love* for us. A long time before this event, Jer 30:19 prophesied that God would confer great significance to the small by glorifying them.

"Being needy" is a hallmark of being human and productive of generating patience and empathy to others in sticky situations. My neediness essentially led to being weaned off reliance on others and turning to God directly—a foreign and terror-filled exercise that can be described as enormous generosity on God's part, as the following narrativized example from Kierkegaard will explain.

De Silentio is the name of the narrative voice in a chapter titled "Attunement" in Kierkegaard's *Fear and Trembling* that has as its central motif the difficult process from the milk to the meat of the word.[24] *De Silencio*, meaning "of silence," fills in some of the silences between the lines of the biblical narrative on Abraham, instructive for this purpose. Here, God is represented as a mother who attempts to disaccustom Abraham from his dependence on a love that manifests by material means. Difficult as it is, God as mother affects a distancing from the child (Abraham/me/the person of faith) in order to wean him off her breast and introduce him to solid food, that is, to a maturity of faith that does not "rest on

---

23. A concept from Agamben, *Coming Community*, 24

24. Heb 5:12–14

the wisdom of men, but on the power of God" (1 Cor 2:5). Weaning could be defined as breaking a pattern of dependence. In this context, weaning turns Abraham towards a conviction in what is unseen, unapparent, and seemingly withdrawn.

Likewise, and associated with dis-habituation, weaning breaks a habit, addiction or dependence, and in addition, outgrows worldly supports that imperil a mature faith. Weaning then is characterized as breaking away from reliance on the sustenance and subsistence that can be seen, felt, and held, symbolized by the breast, toward that which is radically different to it: hope, that the withdrawn breast doesn't necessarily mean a withdrawal of the mother who may appear withdrawn but is nevertheless *present*. Apart from being cast as a maternal figure, God trains her child to be independent: to free him (us) into a trust that does not depend on, and can withstand, the compelling logic and evidence produced by the world. Dependence on the world alone would lead to a perception of the withdrawn breast as a cruel and unnecessary separation, thus changing the child's estimation of the mother (God here) and also obfuscating the imperceptibility of the mother's love. In *De Silencio*'s narrative, Abraham is the greatest example of faith during the Akedah/the sacrifice of Isaac, because he believes God is present despite experiencing God's absence and, in this way, his belief forms a *connection* to God, despite *separation,* referred to as faith.

The transition from presence of the mother to her absence is perilous for both mother and child, for Abraham/you and I are now seemingly alone with only the belief that mother is still *present*. In contrast, a child who believes that it has always been on its own has no choice but to depend on the sustenance that is seen and felt. De Caussade describes this world as habituating a rejection of "the inestimable treasure" that is "concealed."[25] Human limitations are woven into Abraham's faith, not excluded by it, by *De Silencio*, thereby implying the torment Abraham may have endured on that three-day journey into miserable paradox. That is that God's love for Abraham is *present* even though there is no tangible evidence. The torment the experience bestows is ironically justified since

25. De Caussade, *Self-Abandonment*, 74.

the implication is that the mother (parent) who keeps her child dependent on her breast is possessive and impedes the child's free will and maturation. The Divine mother is concerned to *separate* from the child despite the pain and difficulty involved, in order to instill a trust based on a faith that withstands and defeats the adverse circumstances of time and space.

In the case of Abraham/in the case of God the father, love necessitates, among other things, a giving up of what one loves most: they "must hate and betray what is most lovable. Hate cannot be hate, it can only be the sacrifice of love to love," maintains Derrida in the *Gift of Death*. Prior to this Derrida writes, "If I put to death or grant death to what I hate it is not a sacrifice. I must sacrifice what I love."[26] Here Derrida is also attempting to make sense of Kierkegaard's reading of Luke 14:26, when Christ urges a subordination of familial identity formation and self-agenda to love: "If anyone comes to me and does not hate his own father and mother and wife and children and brothers and sisters, yes, and even his own life, he cannot be my disciple." What Derrida appears to be inferring by the title of his book is that the impending death of Isaac and the actual death of Jesus is the gift. The tableau of the fraught Abraham and Isaac on Mount Moriah is interrupted to be completed in the future on the mount of Calvary. God does not request anything of anyone that he does not enact himself. Love then is, among other things, a giving up, or interruption, of what one loves, of what one is culturally and personally and theologically subscribed to, in order to form relations with, and create a place for, those who are different and needy.

Christian love as defined in the New Testament, effectively fractures dependence on identity formations that bind us to hierarchies of preference instituted by the temporal world. Since many of us are unwilling and/or unable to verbalize our needs, misery, and love, or explain our motive for adhering to Divine requests as Abraham did, we can be conceived as interstitial: both in this world and *another*, we are in, though not of, the world which enables the co-inherence of radically different orders and also interpretations

26. Derrida, *Gift of Death*, 64.

of who we are.[27] As vectors where two orders converge, "God leaves him (Abraham and us) free to refuse—and that is the test."[28]

Equally important to the story of faith and love is this, God sees to human, and in this instance, Abraham's needs. In respect to the appointed place where the sacrifice was prevented, "appropriately Abraham names the place *Jahweh-jireh*, 'Yahweh sees (or provides).' He does not call this site 'Abraham-*shama*' (Abraham obeyed)."[29] J. Gerald Janzen casts similar light on this topic in asserting that "the teaching of this mountain in Moriah is that to live within the providence of God is to live within a horizon defined not by our 'seeing' but by God's provision ('pro-vision')."[30]

The church referred to earlier provided a solid conceptual theological grounding; what was required of me was this perilous Abrahamic journey to the heart of lived faith. The church is imperfect, yet like the Christian, redeemed by Jesus. As Beecher observes, "the church is not a gallery for the exhibition of eminent Christians but a school for the education of imperfect ones, a nursery for the care of weak ones, and a hospital for healing of those who need diligent care."[31] All in service to equipping the saints to follow in the steps of the rabbi *extraordinaire*. Of course, the church is much more than can be summarized here. A question for the church broadly sketched in Zechariah is, are we going to become people who, like Jesus, participate in and activate God's agenda?

I became mindful through the ideas of Georgio Agamben, that the Christian God "wants the loved one with all of its predicates, its being *such* as it is."[32] He is indifferent to "this or that property" of the beloved. Being is sufficient for the extraordinary love of God, in whom belonging is not based on any condition, quality, or lack. In turn, Christian love through the church requires parataxis: naked truth *and* love of Christ, *and* generosity, *and* patience, *and*

---

27. The context of Taylor's citation is altered. *Journeys to Selfhood*, 260.

28. Derrida, "Whom To Give To," 165.

29. Hamilton, *Book of Genesis*, 113.

30. Janzen, *Abraham*, 81.

31. DeHaan and Bosch, *Our Daily Bread*, November 6.

32. Agamben, *Coming Community*, 1–2.

integrity, *and* the importance of the fruit of his Spirit in us, . . . and . . . and . . . and . . .

Like most in contemporary culture, lying dormant was a shameful personal desire to experience how it would feel to be very powerful in some way. How does someone like Bill Gates or Angela Merkel feel about themselves and others? Rupert Murdock has global power and control over media, setting political and economic agendas that have far-reaching consequences for national objectives. Have you ever thought about being so beautiful/handsome that people change their behavior around you? In any case, there were no prayers about it, but it did pass through my mind on many occasions.

One morning when standing in front of a university college class, an experience/impression crumpled me for days. In this class, students, both male and female, from various countries in the Middle East sat in the front row. Many wore hijabs and some of the young men too wore traditional religious garb. In the second row sat all the students from various parts of Asia. The third row was occupied by locals and European students. This was a new class, of the world in microcosm, at a different university.

On the morning in question, they had an exam. As the requisites were explained, the most intense experience of superhuman *love* took total possession of me. Again, time stopped as *love* saturated my neighbors through and through: pure, uncontaminated, *Holy love*. Appearance, capabilities, and all marks of distinguishment were subjected to transfiguration. Then, God said, *"this is what it is like to be powerful."* In a timeless instant, *I* was the most powerful person in the world because God's love had suffused me. The feeling was so powerfully sad, grief turned on and off for the next forty-eight hours. Love's power had bypassed time and cut out the discriminatory ways of the world. God is subjected to this crushing of love on an infinite scale when his love is spurned. "I have always loved you," says the Lord. But you retort, "Really? How have you loved us"? (Mal 1:2).

Intense love overshadowed and shook me now and then for many years, in trams, church, home, pubs, and many other places.

Two types of learning were taking place simultaneously during my research: the theoretical and experiential: both on love. The former engaged with the wisdom of the page and the latter taught me how to respect the heart in real time, his, my own and those of others.

Desperately in need of rest from a heavy schedule, on two occasions I had fallen asleep with my eyes open. Exhausted one night, like the giant cockroach Gregor Samsa in Kafka's *Metamorphosis*, I scurried into bed and saw the body of Christ stood large in front of me. His hands were outstretched, inviting me to sleep within him. In his open body was a small chamber with soft light. Instinctively I stepped into him and fell asleep instantly. It brings to mind the line of a hymn, "Rock of Ages cleft for me, let me hide myself in Thee."[33] The next morning the cockroach had gone, but despite a sense of rest I wondered how long two jobs could continue. In the kitchen over morning coffee a few days later, God said, "*it's time to love*," and with this was an invisible line, like a transparent umbilical cord, connected from the center of my chest cavity up into the infinite. Slowly, spirit first, *I* was being taken upwards.

---

33. This is a hymn by Augustus Toplady, entitled "Rock of Ages."

8

Seeing in the Spirit, Being Out of the Spirit to Increasing Manifestations of Fear

THE FIRST SIGHTING OF a heavenly being at about the age of two occurred when Mother's extended family was holidaying together and early that morning, perhaps as a result of very warm weather, all had descended to the river. Later, mother and I were the last to leave as we wandered on lush green grass towards the sound of running water framed by greenery. She was on my left, holding my hand. The angel, who had no wings but was nevertheless airborne and horizontal, was also ahead on my left. It was quite long, tall that is, and it was carrying something small, in both of its hands. It appeared neither male nor female and it had on its face the appearance of what is now recognized as the look of those people who pray a great deal. Their faces contain light as if they are not quite solid. Even though it was in mother's field of vision, she was oblivious. Her profile was still and looking straight ahead. Beautifully preoccupied. How I wish we had shared the angel, just like perhaps

Saint Augustine and his mother Monica who shared a vision.[1] Later fear set in that time would steal that memory in the same way black and white photos are left looking bleached and unreal.

It was around this age on one visit to my maternal grandmother's, she sat me on a chair and conveyed with urgency in her voice, "you must get your name into the Lamb's book of life" (Rev 3:5, ESV). Even then, that speechless two-year-old knew who the Lamb was. That child determined to do what her beloved granny Ivy wanted. Ivy was unaffectionate, never sentimental, with fierce focus folding the areas above her brows like two pleats in a skirt, but her actions articulated the lushness of Ivy's inner life, and I thought often about that book of life, the tree of life, and now, how sheep and lambs are the most defenseless creatures in need of protection.

About ten years ago, I learned through mother's youngest sister living in Sydney that Ivy was an evangelist. She would spend much time translating scriptures from English, writing them on paper and going out into the streets to tell people about Jesus. A solid woman with a commanding intensity, she was a spiritual force to be reckoned with, intrepid and full of faith. She died the morning after I dreamed of her death, at the age of five. Her coffin lay in the living room of her home, where my lips touched her icy forehead which was like a silver metallic bowl that contained ice cream. Cold, empty, and silent, her proximity emitted comfort. Her inviting house, with the voices of life, aromas of exotic food, and garden of delights, was now creepy and drooping. Some of the adults at the funeral sent me to a room where all the other children, my cousins, were playing uproariously, unaware that fear was palpable. Whilst alive, the forces of evil kept a very safe distance from her. After death, creepy crawlies were in full party mode in her home. I escaped outside into the harsh sunlight of mid-morning feeling the separation of her loss.

The next encounter with the supernatural occurred also at the age of five. Working in the army, father was away for long periods of time. Mother had taken elder sister Sue (two-and-a-half years older than me), my six-month-old brother, and myself to stay with

1. Augustine, *Conf.* 9.10.

her elder sister and family. Mum understandably felt safer having company. However, that house and I were not friends. It was downright sinister, containing fear mixed with *something* I could not name, and it engendered screams of fear one night. When not at school, a great deal of time was spent outside playing wonderful imaginary games from real life in preference to being with the other children in the house. Games outside were most welcome. Of most concern was the larger-than-life-sized black aloof Buddha in the living room that was to be ignored at all costs.

The room at the front of that large house was temporarily ours. Mother and her sister's family were at the back of the house. One night, terrified by something in the room, I was unable to move, compelling an inordinate focus on impending danger that restricted efforts to breathe deeply. Sue, in the bed next to me, behind me and close to the wall was sound asleep. Baby brother, directly in front of me, in his cot, was also asleep. A valiant effort was made not to engage with the communication of the darkness, shifting shapes, and sounds in the room. A presence of fear sat like a block of concrete over me, squeezing the breath out of me. Laying there arrested seemed interminable; whatever possessed me to finally turn towards my sister brought to eye several smallish angels with wings, positioned at the head of the bed, two or three stood between us, and a third was at the foot of the bed. About five in all. Sleep fell instantly. Those angels overwhelmed the evil as they stood guard. Experience proves God commands his angels to guard us at all times (Ps 91:11), and "angels are only servant spirits sent to care for people who will inherit salvation" (Heb 1:14).

It was in that house that my older cousins mentioned a man named Charles Manson and the death of Sharon Tate and her unborn child. This news item caused physiological change: icy fear gripped me. When I was older and wiser, there were equally frightening phenomena in the streets and surrounding areas around me, such as the poverty that drove mothers to amputate their children's limbs in order to elicit the generosity of passers' by. One of our neighbors attempted to take her own life several times in the most desperate ways, unsuccessfully. The unneighborly appeared to talk about her, adding humiliation and injury to her impoverishment. Suicide isn't uncommon among the poor. Gossip, the drums of voodoo, wife abuse, and an undercurrent of hopelessness partied all around my childhood. Although forbidden from leaving the house, love of reading was the excuse used to make individual walks to places "out of bounds" for the purposes of procuring books. One short walk one sweltering afternoon presented two people having sex (it wasn't clear what they were doing at the time), in space no larger than a playpen, otherwise called a dwelling made of dilapidated, disposable materials. The road was littered with the poor that bordered on a canal oozing filthy stench. All the wounds of a dismantling world embedded my surroundings. Unprotected from fortified indifference, life outside rattled, honked, fornicated, and suffered. Men in rotten, drooping skirts itched and waddled. Women in saris reflected the sun like mirrors as they carried pots perched precariously on their shiny, long, oiled hair. Their skin like roasted curry powder. Dust was edged into fruit lying on decrepit jute bags that had once transported food from village to metropolis. The temple bells rang to the scent of frangipani. Time to go home.

As you may have guessed, the first ten years of my life was spent in the poor world, euphemistically relabeled the third world which could be romantically characterized as being magical, with a provocative darkness that birthed a sadness that lingers to this day. The beauty of many of its people take the form of kindness, sharing, and innocent openness. While the evils of colonization are justifiable in some instants, Christian missionaries came along with them, bearing the protestant Jesus along with an adequate education in the English language, both invaluable to my life!

Affluent children in the West play games such as cricket, enjoy swimming, and have access to a gamut of pleasurable options. Play with local children pre-school took the form of cooking with real fire and tiny cooking pots which were sold everywhere. Mother would provide the required food. Often Mala and I would sit in the garden, and she would enjoy consuming the food prepared in our little pots as conversation flowed between two languages easily. It is to be expected that those who are constantly hungry would enjoy cooking more than any other game children play in the West. Mala's freedom was restricted by hunger. She did not choose to be born in that country or to an irresponsible father, in a status that would confer an ordinary education that would perhaps keep her functioning in an economy she had little or no access to. The lentils she enjoyed so much became a preferred meal for my son and self, later in Australia. The search for Mala and her siblings continued on return visits, but the heat, tropics, and time have swallowed them up. Prayer is my only connection with them.

By the age of eight the desire to attend church and/or Sunday School had ebbed. To this day, the reason is not clear. Perhaps it was the long walk in the scorching sun to and from church which my sister and I negotiated hesitatingly each Sunday! After that decision, a gradual and progressive unhappiness, irritability, and loneliness moved in and became unwelcome neighbors who would keep me up at night. This is in stark contrast to preschool, and my inner world peopled by God, ants, angels, orchids, and the immense range of unforgettable people, images, and events that made up life as a child. Excitement was courted often as various theological issues presented themselves, such as who created God and why do I need to keep breathing; it's much too much work! Many, many years and landscapes later, many God questions were answered from the safety of Christian conviction. The intervening years of spiritual dereliction almost murdered me.

During the long years before conversion to Christianity, one supernatural event presented in the final year of high school in a room which resembled and smelt like a nicotine den. A group of students, zealous in ambition, began a conversation about their plans for the future. There was a keen primary teacher among us, a businesswoman who was capable of being an academic, and perhaps an accountant. On and on it went, leaving me somewhat bereft. Finally, everyone had spoken, and one of the lads said to me, "What will you do?" Half in jest, came the reply: "Perhaps I will become Buddhist and live in the foothills of the Himalayas." Simultaneously, a visual image of Christ, striking, powerful, and large overwhelmed my mind (and heart) to the point of disabling speech. Instantaneously, absolute certainty conveyed that Buddhism in the Himalayas was not an option. Astounded and bewildered by that experience, the reminder returned of finding some form of transcendent meaning and purpose to my life. Regardless of the vision, philosophy seemed to be the most exciting prospect. Four years later, it had fallen well short of the mark, generating an existential crisis: why live at all if there is nothing but myself?

9

On Life, Death, and the Hound of Heaven

ON THE QUESTION OF life and death, mother often recalls how she saved me from expiring on two separate occasions as a child. Once, breathing stopped from asthma, and on the other, the van we were in lost control and ended up in the murky brown water of a large river. Clear recollection of sinking into cloudy water has remained in the same way mother, who couldn't swim, frantically plunged into the water in hope of finding me. Relentless and crazed groping with her hands in the opaque water found and pulled me out, as she refused to be bullied into submission by that force of nature that was immeasurably larger and stronger than herself. Each time, she had me resuscitated and brought back. She argues to this day that these incidents were miraculous. In times of trial, which were regularly, however, I have often wished she had not tried so hard or perhaps not at all.

It is true to say, without going into detail, that much of my life was lived in fear, at times extreme fearfulness. As a child home was a fearful place; school was a refuge, and education was a haven until 2013. Childhood trailed alongside me and behind me, unreachable, and annexed by images and people that imposed estrangement. Engagement with the page at school appeared to be my only consolation. One much older girl at school on two or three separate occasions unbarred my cage when she said of me, "Oh, she is lovely," and it made an immense difference, like Joseph being pulled out of that pit, Daniel from the lions. In those moments, I saw myself as an inner photo like an x-ray was taken of someone alive and faintly lovely.

By the age of twenty, life was unsettling and unstable, nomadic qualities sprouted vigorously to pilot escape from desolation. The realization of searching for *something* for a very long time was half married to a vagueness of discovering it. That thread had been lost by the age of twenty-six. Since, life had become alien, sapping my strength. The central books of other faiths were explored, eventually re-turning to the Bible, the Old Testament in fact, but it made no sense and had absolutely no meaning and was tantamount to trying to scale an infinite brick wall without a foothold. Through education some -isms were grafted: socialism, feminism, criticism, give-in-ism. Finally, after thinking a great deal about my circumstances, there was nothing left to explore. Undertaking preliminary honors in politics at university at the time meant nothing. Devoid of all desire and expectation, that girl with the withdrawn face in her homemade deep, dark, sea green skirt, in a photo taken at the time, hurtled through nothingness in slow motion, with every cell of promise rebelling against itself.

On the day life would end, the morning dragged on endlessly. Finally, a 5:00 p.m. tutorial in politics reluctantly beckoned to defeat the interminable wait. It was winter and a persistent rain had worn out its welcome. Daylight turns into darkness around 5:00 p.m.-ish. Just before leaving for university at about 4:15 p.m., the low grey sky through my bedroom window was scanned as I cried silently in desperation: *"God if you exist, help me."*

I dressed in full black, not because it was fashionable in Melbourne. Rather, all the clothes owned was also subjected to a black vortex, but for one exception, the delicate shoes on my feet were white, strangely. The tutorial banged on like Hare Krishna's lost in an esoteric paradise when existence itself was dubious. An inviting park bench caught in the drizzle between the Menzies Building and the Union Building on the campus of Monash University was as good a place as any to park my worries. It's a mystery how long the dark ensconced me until a small voice on the left of me said, "God loves you," and another voice on the right of me said, "Jesus loves you." An implosion in my solar plexus injected a huge dose of life into every part of my sad carcass and my intellect sang and bowed to: God actually exists! Tucking the evidence for the existence of God firmly into my resuscitated heart were two young African-American students with painted white faces who had come all the way from Harlem, USA, and sat on either side of me like exotic archangels. While performing with a Christian group on campus, they had seen me. I have something unpleasant to confess, it is not coincidental that these two girls had been brought all the way from the United States to kickstart my heart. Apparently, they did not receive airline tickets until the eleventh hour struck a generous donor. Back then, if an Anglo Caucasian person told me about God, the result may have been doubtful, as my siblings, particularly brother and self, suffered painfully on occasion in Australia because we seemed to be the only migrants around at the time that were not entirely European. Having said that, to me and many others, the visual Jesus was Anglo Caucasian, the conceptual Jesus was Semitic. Later, these two intertwined into the knowable yet ineffable *One*.

I recall levitating, truly legless, on the way home that faithful night filled with unimaginable excitement, just as it was in a small village in Bethlehem Ephrathah when an extraordinary baby was born.

Granted, whoever calls on the Lord will be saved (Rom 10:13), and my name is already inscribed in the Lamb's book of life after all, before the foundation of the world, and for reasons unknown.

Then the difficulties began, as it does for many Christians, invariably interrupted by the incredible and incredulous. A few weeks later, at 5:00 p.m. in the evening I stood between the automatic doors of the campus center not having eaten all day and absentmindedly thought, *God I would love a coffee.* Instantly a male student walked through the doors and said, "I will buy you a coffee if we can talk about the essay." Yet, like the exodus in the desert who forgot they were on their way to the promised land, so much time was wasted that could have been used by God for his purposes. Faithful to the faithless, Father disciplined me with one hand and comforted me with the other until over a long period of time later, he was asked by me why he had bothered. His patience, spelled l-o-v-e, was/is taking shape on a human tapestry, each cross stitched painstakingly and consummately on a visible web of square holes. Who else would have stayed to cover my nudity with the inventiveness of so many colorful crosses?

10

Satan Is a Shadow of Himself

WHILE SINGLE, NOT LONG after conversion, the evil one manifested with a child under each arm. One of the children was identified as my sister's elder son who, about five years old at the time, was having very strange experiences that terrified him and the rest of the family. Whenever he fell asleep, he would feel an evil presence and would have his eyes open, while being unresponsive and catatonic, such that, he was neither asleep nor awake. The other child was not identified. In the vision, my nephew was saved through Jesus, but the other child remained in Satan's clutches. It was not until my own son was five or six years old that the other child was recognized as my own.

At the time, his behavior was disturbing for reasons that will not be discussed. There was only one way to rescue him from the clutches of evil, and me from torment: through Christ. One night whilst sitting on the edge of my futon, Christ manifested in front of the evil one and simultaneously, the fiend dropped my child down instantly. Jesus stooped down, picked him up and gently placed him in my hands.

It may now be a cliché, but the enemy will attack and try to destroy what is most loved in life. Whether it is a person or people, a goal, a desire, a triumph, and especially our love of God. Over the years it has been proven time and again that love is that which can move the impossible, multiply food even in supermarket trolleys, carry burdens, revolutionize the human heart, renovate the mind, and recreate lives. Majestically proclaimed by 1 Cor 13:8, love always succeeds. This Scripture works even with difficult people who hate Christians. Why, may you ask? Because of Saint John's ontological declaration: God is love itself (1 John 4:8, 16). For this reason, every exercise and expression of love actualizes God manifestly. Hence the attacks over millennia to victimize and exterminate love.

When we encounter situations where we must defend our faith and ourselves, the loving approach is to call out lies, deception, and persecution. Spiritual warfare is necessary when we fight the good fight with the fruit of the spirit to reveal the truth, even if this means going to court. Saint Paul instructs in Phil 1:28, "Don't be intimidated in any way by your enemies," and Ps 37:15 exclaims that they will fall on their own swords. Persecution of Christians appears to have reached critical mass in the United Kingdom, sparking *Christian Concern*, an organization supporting persecuted Christians taken to court.

The prophetic dream that follows best encapsulates the necessity of pushing back against maltreatment. In presenting food of various kinds that looked tantalizingly delicious, and unrefusable, the tiered cake and its icing became the focus of the dream. Nefariously seductive in its many layers oozing soft icing and irresistible in appearance, it would be served to my family, well aware that it was composed of human excrement. My earthly father, signifying my heavenly father, stepped in. Praises of the cake were halted to an abrupt albeit kindly directive: "Do not eat waste in any disguise despite how good it looks." The dream ended with nausea as all the food discarded in the bin really was repulsive. Work is important to sustain our families as the food in the dream signified, but not when work enforces ill treatment motivated by persecution that has the effect of contaminating the food it provides.

The second encounter with Satan occurred many years later in about 2005 or 2006. He stood at the foot of our bed, up close and grossly violating my space. Second husband Geoff was asleep and had no idea. Paralyzed with fear to the point that even Jesus was not called, the fiend looked the same as he did in his debut visit, yet this time, convincingly made his intimidating presence felt over what appeared to be an extended period of time.

The next encounter was recently, in 2021. Over a few weeks at night while asleep, something would blow on my face at point blank range to wake me up. Perplexing and strange, Satan made an appearance after the final of these experiences which was quite pronounced, like a drum roll. This time, despite the flamboyant entrance, he only materialized partially as a parody of himself, and instantly disappeared like a puff of smoke. Unnerving? No, though somewhat amusing. Prior to this incident and repeatedly, the following Scripture took root and burst into flower in real life: "The God of peace will soon crush Satan under your feet" (Rom 16:20) in a manner descriptive of Ps 37:20, the Lord's enemies will disappear like smoke. Scriptures quite literally nailed in the present!

This is quite remarkable given that, seven to ten years ago, anxiety and fear would break in through the night just as Old Nick (Satan) had done in 2021. A racing heart would follow like an athlete jumping the gun and handing the baton to constriction of breath, inability to think clearly, and physical pain in the center of my being. Life was lived as a race to evict anxiety by keeping busy.

Giving up my job at the university in 2013 commenced a two-year wilderness period of struggling through finances, unemployment, the prospect of no future, and intense anxiety burning day and night. Peace tangoed with acute apprehension to distort focus. The dance would turn into a knockout, no-holds-barred competition which would pendulate between believing that God was unable to change my situation, as well as a faith that God would. Fear and faith fluctuated until clarity and lucidity declared faith a temporary winner until the next time. While locked in this battle, the Holy Spirit, residing within, generally and specifically intercedes on our behalf (Rom 8:26–27). One night full of inner conflict, I plummeted into an infinite spiritual depth within until the spirit jarringly broke my fall and instantly brought me back to this life. On another wilderness night while thinking about a story John Smith[1] had related, in a desperate bid to be out of the swarming vicissitudes of the desert, I asked Jesus to hold me. As soon as sleep fell, he held me for a prolonged time. John Smith told me of a friend who, while ill, had his feet sponged by Jesus as he sat on his bed.

Faith would not be faith if it were not accompanied by and overcame fear. These two are archrivals on two fronts in the story of one of the greatest biblical warriors, Joshua. In paving a way to and securing the promised land, he was embattled by fear, judging from the countless times he is told "do not fear." Gideon and Moses required repeated reassurance before, during, and after each mission. Abraham before the sacrifice of Isaac was fickle in faith, particularly in matters relating to his spouse. To a man who was perennially on the frontline, some of the Psalms written by David are the Old Testament version of the protective armor of God outlined in Ephesians 6, enabling him "to withstand in the evil day, and having done all, to stand," by praying unceasingly. Prayerful Psalms and songs outflanked David's fear. Ezekiel hid in a cave and in fear, Peter abandoned Jesus. These cowards were used mightily when experiential knowledge of God's support replaced fear.

The wilderness is a place of extreme temperature and landscape, largely inhospitable to human habitation, but can also be characterized as a place of wandering (Exod 16:1), desolation (Jer 22:6; Matt 3:1–3) and exile (Exod 12:41); it is also the place of God's provision (Deut 2:7), guidance (Ps 78:52), and mighty acts (Ps 78:15–16). In Jer 31.3, the wilderness is a place where the Israelites found grace. In Hos 2:14, God "allures" Israel into the wilderness that he may "speak kindly to her." In the New Testament, the wilderness is where Christ resists temptation, and feeds

---

1. Smith ministered to Hell's Angels Bikies, who then became the God Squad.

five thousand with a few pantry essentials at that time: bread and fish. It is moreover, the place where two prophets, Isaiah and John the Baptist, preach and prepare the way for the Messiah in order that "all flesh shall see the salvation of God" (Luke 3:4–6). In these Scriptures, the wilderness marks a difficult transition to a state that is *other* than worldly. The wilderness experience prompts giving up of what one loves (in my case the security and pride that came from my job), of what one is bound to (self primarily), in order to form relations with, and create a place for, God's agenda that, cultivates a wider sense of responsibility.

Faith becomes central in desert conditions and instigates an unending battle with the senses in order to develop a discernment not conclusively based on what is apparent. I was being weaned from my dependence on self and the world; a process Jean Pierre de Caussade captures so very accurately: "God leaves the individual without any other support than himself alone. It feels its necessities and miseries without knowing how or when it will be helped."[2] The implication is, in faith or trust, one feels orphaned, unable to identify with the familiar world of reason, sight, and sound, and in the same instant, uncertain of that which one is turned toward. Orphanization is derived from the Greek *orphanos*, which the Oxford Dictionary translates as "bereaved," meaning "deprived of relation." The difference with me was a supportive, prayerful spouse.

Precipitating crippling anxiety, the wilderness was untenable. A serious and desperate word with the almighty ensued: could he *please* either deliver me from anxiety or rid me of this mortal coil? On arrival at church on the Sunday after that prayer, there was a bottle of oil on a table. The Spirit disclosed I should ask for prayer. A woman of God and healer laid hands on me and took me back to the first experience of anxiety as a child. This time, she asked Jesus to reach out, take my hand, and control the situation. She anointed my head with oil. That night, although sleep was broken several times, there was no break-in.

---

2. De Caussade, *Self-Abandonment*, 81.

During the wilderness experience, like Elisha's servant, the Lord opens our eyes to look up to him and see the powerful panoramic support from heavenly hosts (2 Kgs 6:17).

Many years prior, whilst living in that wonderful flat referred to earlier, post-traumatic stress triggered and raised to the surface many terrible experiences from childhood. The worst aspect of these was the perpetrator enjoying inflicting fear in me. On a walk early one morning a storm of memories ran amok, so much so that my head was no longer above water. Usually, one awful memory at a time is revealed, thanks to the grace that permits process. This morning however, a flood of images, narratives, taunts, fear, pain and suffering abducted me. The air was butchered by the beast of memory; fear cuts, hurts, shrieks, and turns back the hands of time to immunize against the intrusive sounds of happiness. Childhood ghosts had come stalking and stuck like shards of sharp glass to the present. One thought cut into this manmade storm: *only you can set me free of this, Jesus.* Over a year later, on another crisp early morning walk, God had healed me so completely that morning, the realization came one year later. The memories were there, but they caused no pain or splitting. With that rescue came a real sense of safety and even a love for the central perpetrator of my childhood fear, to the extent that it is no longer justifiable to recount those childhood experiences.

11

Come to *Me!*[1]

WHILE TRAVELING TO PRAYER group one night, in a split second a small rock was noticed before it landed on the windscreen, centimetres from my face. The word *God* was uttered silently, and the worst expected. The sound of crashing glass was heard, yet there wasn't even a dent on the windscreen, and my face was intact!

Composed of three people, the prayer group that formed at a church attended about ten years ago would swell to include whoever turned up on the night.

Late one night, a youngish man got out of prison, into a taxi, scaled the seven-foot fence and joined the startled prayer group. He arrived, knelt before us with humble hands outstretched, voiceless, eyes shut, emaciated. His youth and good looks prompted awful thoughts of what may have been endured in prison. The spirit lifted these prayer warriors to a different level that night. Faltering, his voice returned at the end of prayer to inform us he had nowhere to go to that night. A man who frequently attended prayer group made a very generous offer of his own place for a few days. Previously, this voiceless man was different; he had a habit of

---

1. Specifically Ps 50:15.

stealing from the offering plate. When I first saw him pick up the money I dropped into the plate, anger resulted. After alerting senior staff, I went to the loo, where my anger was met by a question from the Spirit: "*who did you give that money to*"? I got it, God can do anything with his money. A high-security option was adopted by the church so it could not happen again. To me it is now clear: God was trying to keep him out of prison.

On a different night, a man of about thirty-five, laconic and withdrawn, gave the prayer group his testimony of an encounter he once had with Jesus. Although quite private and with difficulty, he related how, in a dream or vision Jesus took him into his arms, just like a mother cradles her infant, and simply rocked him. This experience kept this man alive after having lost his mother as an infant and his father's continual mistreatment.

One of the three members of the prayer group named Sharon shared a story that had occurred a few years prior. Having been cursed, serious illness followed. In fact, after examination in hospital she was told that all her organs were shutting down. She only had a couple of days to live. Before her time was up, an enormous angel stood in front of her, placed its hands into her body, and asserted, "by his stripes you are healed."[2] She was. She also related how a car collision was averted when an angel stuck its hands through her windscreen and took control of her car.

A brother from a religious order who lived near the church in government housing would, when invited, tell us about his life. An artist of considerable talent, Brother P's loneliness was just as extensive. At times, while having a cup of tea in his tiny, lonely kitchen, Jesus would join him at his wooden table!

On one occasion many years ago, while researching in the library, a call came through from a friend met in a Christianity explained course. Previously a medical doctor in the emergency unit of a large Beijing hospital, she was unable to find work in Melbourne for three years as a consequence of her English language skills, which were not up to sitting the entrance exam to practice medicine in Australia. Applications for research positions

2. Isa 53:5.

were submitted instead. On leaving a theological library to pick up James from school, on a tram ride which would take fifteen minutes, she called and said she was suicidal because she could not find work. Three years is a long time to be out of work for someone who was intelligent and educated, generous and warm. Married with a son a few years younger than my own, she was also a new Christian. Fervent prayer followed, aware of the seriousness of the situation. On hopping off the tram, she called again. Via email she had received a job offer undertaking research at a university. She was now triumphant, and God had just made me a part of another sensational answer to a complex request.

Later, whilst in prayer one morning, a vision of the above woman occurred. She stood looking surprised, in the middle of a meadow on a spring day, illuminated by sunshine and surrounded by butterflies. Not long after this experience, she moved interstate. I have not heard from her since.

A single woman for about twelve years after divorce and having made mistakes in dating men, two or three over that time as it turned out, the right fit had alluded me. Prayer was honest and not so urgent. Unable to imagine dating again, it was communicated that if he wanted me to be with someone, could the person be brought to me? I would not go out looking for anyone, and could the person please see me through his eyes?

In 2005, a man who was not known well, but employed by the church, rang me and came over to, he said, "return something I had left at church camp." He sat at the dining table of that blessed flat with his face turned towards that glorious view and related his feelings for me. He explained that he would like to date me specifically with a view to marriage. At the time, he had no idea he was fulfilling a prayer. We were married later that year. His two sons were already acquainted with my own through church. With all certainty this was the man God had selected for me because of that prayer, and the other miracle is he most often sees me through Christic eyes. In fact, he has had the greatest effect on me by example and the fact that the gospel lives through him. He has spent much time in prayer for me: the greatest gift any human has given me.

Yet another inexplicable response to prayer occurred after my son celebrated his eighteenth birthday in April by inviting a few friends' home. As the only adult there, food was provided while also remaining out of sight in the front room, ensuring all was well. All the young people invited were completing their final year of schooling. Throughout the evening from the living room, among the sounds of chatter, music, and laughs, came the sound of a girl coughing incessantly. The spirit led me in prayer for her. It is fair to say, she was of concern. After they left, my son was asked about her. Apparently, Maggie (not her real name) had cystic fibrosis, which was responsible for the lack of breath that generated the cough.

Just before the first end of school exams began in October, James broke the news that she had passed away from cystic fibrosis. Shock and sadness raced ahead of me, coupled with a feeling of frustration at meager efforts to intercede for her. Prayer requests for her became quite obsessive-compulsive, haranguing God because of my own inadequacy. One morning on the sofa at quiet time, with every intention of raising the issue yet again, God joyously announced, "*Maggie is with me.*" That's all that was needed!

When life is interrupted adversely, we are reminded to seek clarification and to honour the one who sees and hears all, beckoning us to entrust all to him.

More than six years ago an appointment for prayer for myself was organized at the charismatic church in Vermont, that had become my own. As referred to earlier, early childhood was subjected to fear and one of these two prayer sessions revealed what in part was already known. To protect myself as a child, an aspect of me had become quite fierce and this was heightened after the birth of my son, perhaps to protect him. It became evident that another personality, female, young, but extremely strong, was my first line of defense throughout my life and during prayer it was time for her to go. In fact, over some time this aspect of my personality appeared unnecessary and redundant because of increasing spiritual maturity. Almost immediately following these revelations through prayer, a vision took hold, inside the house lived in as a child, standing facing the shut double front doors to the outside. Both doors opened as Jesus walked in, in brilliant light, and knelt on one knee in front of me, smiling joyfully. He held out his hands to the girl and she only had astonished eyes for him. Whilst a part of myself had gone, there was a lucid sense of freedom. Most memorable apart from a shining-with-goodness-God, was the look of release on her face when she went toward him without a sideward glance at me!

On several occasions in prayer while feeling Job-esque, God was asked in the same way Job did, why he created me. He made himself heard immediately, always with the same response: "*for Jesus.*" Aren't all Christians made for him? So it seems in Rom 11:36 (ESV): "For from him and through him and to him are all things."

Poemic Prayers:

Not a puppeteer, a potter,
shaping grace into use,
re-formed in-situ
under protest at the potter's firmness:
Masterpieces beautified in a furnace

You Are

in the wisdom of the ages, the elements, minutiae of days, between moments, in nature's songs, and the weeping lament of love, of loss . . .
You speak
the language of humans, birds, animals and the sea; the light and dark cannot silence you, and
your voice is in solidarity with the humble, truth, . . .
You look
like joy, dignity in poverty, the solidity of patience, hope in loss, and trust in suffering . . .
You come
between time and its end, over and over again . . .

12

The Past Ten Years
From Wilderness to Oasis to Suffering:
Before the Promised Land

HAVING ASKED REPEATEDLY OVER the years if God would employ me, I gave up my job at the university. An urgency to work my faith became critical. Subsequently, our family would have been homeless had we not received an inheritance from my husband's mother passing away, as he was only employed part-time. Over the following two excruciating years, God readjusted my spiritual foundations. Voracious visits, incursions, and involvement with the Prophets, Psalms, Gospels, and Christian poetry and literature was accompanied by fasting and long silences with the Spirit who inspired these books. Poverty was experienced on two fronts: of a spiritual nature, and the materials for life were threadbare. Guilt was a result of living on donations proffered by an aunt in Sydney who was generous and enabled payments to continue for my foster child. In truth, God insisted on maintaining commitment to that child when I had no income. There was no other option than to surrender control and wait on/for/with/through him.

During this time, life was charged with supernatural experiences. In a dream or encounter one night, the Holy Spirit took me back in time to a cave. There were many young people in the cave in dress similar to Jesus' time: a full, midi dress belted at the waist. The Spirit stood close by me on my right, and while I couldn't see the Spirit, his voice was loud, clear, distinct, and delighted as it said, "These are the saints, and a little later, here is Saint Paul," when a young man with a shock of dark hair approached. The atmosphere was one of excitement, energetic activity, and conviviality. Later, the enormity of what was experienced made sense. Those young people in the cave shouldered a revolution that would go on to create the world anew. That was the contagious buzz sensed there. Several days later the book of Acts revealed how the believers were scattered, and some disciples stayed in caves, including later, when Saint Paul traveled widely.

For some time in my wilderness wanderings, there was sense of an encounter, and one afternoon, while sitting in a chair in the living room, freezing, with the Bible opened at Ps 1, Jesus dropped in and through. Young, joyful, and full of bouncy life, the dull, old living room was transformed into a flurry of *other worldliness*. With him was the child I had aborted. As they walked ahead, with his hand in a contemporary gesture, Jesus motioned to me to follow. Up I leapt, sprinted towards him, caught up, threw my hands around his waist and was seized by *pure Joy*, to such an extent that, for the next week, people asked about it, having noticed a fundamental *something* about me. Towards the end of the week, joy started seeping out, though a residue remained permanently. I am a living witness to Ps 16:11, "In his presence there is fullness of joy," and Heb 1:9, the Father "poured out the oil of joy [on him], more than anyone else." Not long after that encounter, a job in a spiritual field was conferred to me. Sir Joy was my new employer: a true radical who was capable of anything, lock, stock, and impossible barrel! This work was the humblest and moreover, intensely purposeful and fulfilling. Christlike virtues fruited and were sown back into the elderly people who were served and loved.

That child with him, my child, visited one Mother's Day prior to the above vision, and asked me *not to send him away just yet.*

Since, he has revisited through a dream. My dream is to be reconciled with him one day!

Voluntary work was taken up in an aged care center while rather baffled by my circumstances. While driving there in thick traffic one morning, God was asked what was going on through an internal conversation: "God, I don't understand. One day I am teaching some of the brightest students in the state and the next I am caring for people with dementia"?

His reply was instant: "I can find a million people to replace you at the university, but I can't find anyone to work with those suffering from dementia."

Moved and humbled, my reply was, *I will do it Lord!*

In the Residential Aged Care Centre that morning, one of the residents who had not spoken for eleven years, woke up, took a look at me, and called. She talked to me at length. She was a Syrian Christian, an academic who had lived in a refugee camp for five years. No one believed me at first, but later, she also talked to others, and her two sons who worked in medical fields thought, as relayed to a mutual source, their mother speaking after eleven years was a miracle. There was no doubt at all! It was God's thank you to her and me.

After receiving an inheritance early in my wilderness journey, we wondered and asked if Jesus wanted us to work overseas. Uncertain, we traveled to three continents, Asia, the Middle East, including Israel, with the final stop being Greece. It was on one particular flight, having woken up when everyone else was asleep, Jesus walked towards me down the aisle. He looked down at me smiling and instantly prompted motivation to pray for Saudi Arabia with immense insight of the Spirit. Opening my eyes, however long later, they fell on the flight path which was on the big screen not very far away. The plane had been flying directly over Saudi Arabia, an enormous, seemingly barren landscape, and prayer for that nation came from above. What a prize! Sleep came while savoring the appearance of him walking calmly down the aisle towards me, not as well-dressed as the cabin crew.

Another Spirit-inspired idea was to list every nation of the world on small pieces of paper, fold each up, and have them all in a jar. Often, my hand plunged into that jar and prayer would follow for the nation in hand. Not so strangely on reflection, one archipelago was selected repeatedly despite the number of other nations in that bowl. A Google search revealed it was devoid of humans, which was perplexing. Had God got it wrong? I did ask why repeated prayer was required. The answer came later. The name of that archipelago is the Spratly Islands in the South China Sea that, unbeknownst to anyone at the time, was being requisitioned by China, now giving them superior advantage on a strategic shipping route.

At this time, about seven years ago in 2014, attendance at a Charismatic Service enriched my spiritual life through an increase in visions, particularly during worship. Many here believed in and were experiencing God in ways that had become familiar to me and the compulsion to conceal extraordinary supernatural encounters became unnecessary. Healings followed. Chest infections, back soreness, and more were healed just being present at worship. Visions followed hot on each other's heels.

In one Jesus was hanging on his cross, it was late afternoon, and dusk was falling rapidly. I was the only one with him and I realized later that I was in the spiritual rather than physical realm. It was apocalyptic. All manner of evil, from the earth, sky, air, and everywhere, were flying into him at lightning speed and determinedly as he breathed his last. I hid behind his cross as the environment all around me was filled with evil indiscriminately entering Jesus. Although dystopian, painful, and inspiring great fear and disquiet, the scene in this vision demonstrated the incredible power of God the Father and the Holy Spirit to resurrect him from that infestation of evil. It wasn't surprising that he believed the Father had abandoned him because Jesus' body at crucifixion had become the site for all the evil in the seen and unseen world, which was defeated just as comprehensively.

In another vision I looked into my own spirit where Jesus, with skirt hitched up and sleeves folded above the elbow, was ankle deep in sticky, black muck. My muck. He was cleaning me up on the inside and looked up at me with the most beatific smile. What a friend we have in Jesus!

Yet another experience in worship was the paralysis of my right hand. Concern was almost immediately assuaged because of a sense that the experience was indeed spiritual rather than physical. When asked what was happening, God replied immediately, "*I am your right hand.*" This was taken by me to mean that he would help me through difficulties, guide me and give me strength as in Pss 89:13 and 138:7. As well as Ps 16:11 (ESV), "At your right hand there are pleasures for evermore." Paralysis of the right hand happened a second time to remind me he was ever-present, as my spiritual care of the elderly began to consume me.

During worship on yet another occasion, Jesus walked up to me with a bunch of keys, and stupidly I refused his offer, asking if he would heal my son instead. After realizing his possible offense at rejection of such a great gift, my heart was sorely challenged and racked by regret. I wondered if he would? Weeks later in quiet time before work, he approached with the keys again and they were taken from him with jubilation. He wasn't asked what they were for. Knowing that they were keys related to the kingdom was sufficient at the time. Forgiving and generous to a fault, his sweetness is contagious and elderly people at work identified his sweetness in me at times. This is quite marvelous as no one would ever refer to me as sweet, being more inclined to Sisyphus of Greek mythology. One of the keys given to me is a mandate to pray for people, places, situations, and circumstances as well as an incredible ability to read the spirits of people. Mostly it is their great sadness that is sensed, but there was one whose hardness was repulsive, causing me to turn away feeling physically stressed. Pride, gluttony, and other traits as well as spiritual virtues are also sensed. Spiritual discernment is what it possibly is. Added on the same ring were keys to unlock various doors which are still being discovered. Exploration is coming through prayer and by simply asking God to reveal them.

A year after starting work with the elderly and a week before a holiday on a Greek Island, on a speed walk, my right ankle was injured. The pain was instant and so was the swelling. A crack in my foot was heard as I went down. The walker who was nearby sidled up to ask if he could call an ambulance. My heart was doing the thinking when holding my foot in my hands, I answered, "I am going to pray for my foot and then walk home on it." His expression was strange. And it came to pass with the first step in faith, the pain was excruciating, but as faith kicked in, each step after that first, was less painful. By the time James prayed that evening, my foot had healed by 60 percent. After he prayed, it was healed 85 percent, and on Sunday, one of the women in church detected some sensitivity and prayed again. Within a week, when that plane lifted into the air for Greece, my foot was healed 97 percent. As Jesus once told his disciples in Mark 5:36, "Just believe."

The Greek Islands became holiday destinations. The next year we took holidays in Chios since our time in Kythera the previous year had been magnificent. From our balcony on the beach in Chios we could see Turkey and decided to pay a day visit to Izmir which required a ferry ride as well as a bus ride once on the coast.

Very small and compact, the ferry allowed two vehicles, a van and a car, to board despite no space for them to park. Both were damaged. Already bottom heavy before the two vehicles, that small vessel bent like a bow after the storm hit. Husband Geoff and I sat on a small upper deck that had a view into the captain's cabin as well as all around the ocean. We were just holding on until a group of about four to five students who were feeling seasick joined us. Rising up high and diving down deep, the small craft battled against the weather conditions. One could sense the fear, even of the captain. One of the young boys vomited all over the table and chairs and we had to move because the vomit was moving with the ferry to map the trajectory of a torrent. Stepping down gingerly onto the only other deck, in front of the vehicles, dark woollen wet arms held on for dear life. Fervent intercession began as the ocean moved into the boat, moving that light container up and down and side-to-side, like an overresponsive marionette.

Manically, Geoffrey wafted around the tiny ferry miraculously taking photos. People react differently! He wasn't afraid because he was too busy being creative. Conditions deteriorated further until the inevitable was sensed: we would all drown. Quietly an SOS was sent to Jesus: "*please, please be with me as I drown.*" Instantly he replied because I knew in my knower that this was not the day to sink. There was also a sense the ferry would arrive safely because of my intercession from the time the storm introduced itself. The trip took double the time to reach Turkey, drenched, salty, triumphal, and unsteady on my feet.

While in Izmir our plan was to visit a street of synagogues that was close to the bazaar where we would be dropped off by the bus. We searched high and low and round and round, not discovering even one. Not wanting to draw attention to ourselves by inquiring from a native, finally we were compelled to. One small synagogue had survived on a derelict outer street, and it was locked up. Whilst peering in through the windows, a young man emerged and asked if we wanted to go in for a price—we did. Clean as a pin, quite small, and with an incredible presence, the scriptural inscription writ large on a wall, although now flushed from memory, filled me with great sadness. The thought of the Jews holding on to their/our God in stormy seas over millennia and despite dispossession and innumerable trials, produced emotional pain in me, while many other questions sailed through my mind. Where are all the Jews in this area today (2018)? Where were all the other synagogues? Did the worshipers of this synagogue lose their lives or were they forced to flee? Where had all the Jews gone? By this time there were lots of males gathering curiously outside the synagogue and both my husband and I felt an urgent need to leave as quickly as possible. Visibly upset, my head stayed down as a very quick escape followed, lest we were benignly detained in the way we had been in another Middle Eastern country a few years previously.

Preliminary research indicated there are just over a couple of thousand Jews living in Izmir. Overall, in Turkey, among other factors, a wealth tax on non-Muslims in the early twentieth century, migration to Israel after 1948 and to a lesser extent anti-Semitism resulted in significant retreat.

The ride back to Chios took just thirty minutes, half the usual time, and the ferry glided very fast on the still water. "He calmed the storm to a whisper and stilled the waves. What a blessing was that stillness as he brought them (us) safely into harbor"! (Ps 107:29–30).

About two months after arriving in Melbourne, while watching the news we heard a ferry had capsized between Chios and the Turkish coast.

As Ps 107 reminds the reader, all of history, including the history of the Jews and my own history, demonstrate the faithful love of God. However, in the most recent vision, a life-sized hourglass contained, held, and rapidly released time, with the sense that *history is running out*. Months later, a second vision of a different much smaller hourglass confirmed the spotlight was on time as finite and fragile.

13

The Christian Front Line
In Dreams/In Reality

During the cold of one wilderness night, a dream, truly disturbing unfolded that could be referred to as the Christian front line. In the form of a line of faithful Christians standing up against the onslaught against the whole body of Christ, the front line was only just holding up under fierce warfare to the detriment of the lives of other Christians and their families who could only live behind the protection of those frontline fighters. Our families were not doing well. For example, even though James was happy, he and other children were playing in the mud and all our families were living rough in difficult environmental conditions.

Seven years later, in 2020, another dream ensued. This time, the front line merited its name as with great effort it was pushing forward slowly to take new ground. Spiritual enemies were being pushed back under heavy fire, with me among the frontline fighters. Christians are defending their faith more successfully, suggesting that God's supernatural giant of a body is waking up, each to the destiny and purpose of role and calling. Fighting the good fight effectively bombards the evil empire into retreat.

There are innumerable front lines in all fields of endeavor and every walk of life. Christian frontliners are intent on defending, and being used by, Christ. They are not career-minded or seek renumeration; instead they serve and sacrifice, surrendering to call and purpose. A colorful example of a successful frontline accessible to all is the Christian apologists and polemicists on YouTube.[1] Impressive in unity and comprised of Christians and ex-Muslims who, while facing great provocation, relentlessly uphold their truth, with unflappable courage, calm, study, and understanding. On other work sites, there may be just one valiant frontliner defending godly virtues and/or the laws of the land and in so doing, pushing against entropy.

In reality, the experience of being on a real front line was demanding while delighting and drawing on all spiritual resources. In the garden of spiritual delights come attacks. One worsened in severity to the point of necessitating challenge. On reflection, the cause of the attack of lies, deception, and distortion was spiritual, yet oddly my spirituality was viewed by the attacker as superfluous. Loving relationships and trust nurtured over a long period of time was the main cause: the green beast of jealousy no less. Of great perplexity was why some Christians who could have been supportive, joined in the persecution. The amazing thing here is the whole sorry mess was brought to a close, without a doubt. That ministry is fondly remembered as corresponding to the baskets of abundance that gratitude and love harvested from the crumbs of my spirit. Sufficiently self-vacated both during and after that ministry, the Master moved in with all manner of spiritual gift to share. His spiritual pampering was/is very well received.

During the intensity of the battle, a vision occurred in my office at that workplace. In it, carrying a very heavy wooden cross over my back as I walked, my heart and mind questioned why it was happening since nothing had been done to warrant it. On the contrary! Just then Jesus walked up alongside me on my right, took

---

1. See the YouTube channels of J. Smith, *Pfander Films*, and Daniel Brubaker, *Variant Quran*.

the heavy cross off me, stuck it in the ground, and said, "I didn't deserve my cross either."

So that was it, a confirmation the cross was being carried for others and that provided immeasurable comfort and courage.

Another vision towards the end of that ordeal occurred during prayer time. Flying in pitch darkness, extremely fatigued and wanting to land desperately, I could not see to negotiate my landing, but then there he was, Jesus carrying a lamp in either hand and communicating to me to either land in front of him or in him. Flight was so rapid that the landing took place with force in front of him, then in him. No interpretation required here!

As persecution raged against me, one morning during prayer time before work, twice Jesus whispered in my left ear that he loved me. It was audible in the breathless silence of reception! This whisper released a healing balm through me, and a layer of safety over me as spiritual fortification.

14

Of the Christian, Christianity, and Christianized West

SOME CHRISTIANS, MYSELF INCLUDED, are somewhat like a vision I once refused to enter, of a shrouded house in darkness, spookily built into and partially camouflaged by a seemingly solid, squat mountain, as in the *Hobbit*. Several times the grossness of the surroundings and façade discouraged me from opening the door and entering. I recoiled from what I imagined was inside. Finally, after several approaches and since it was a vision, with great trepidation, the door was ever so gently opened, only for me to stand mesmerized by complete rose gold surroundings emitting soft light, cast in rounded and arched architecture, utterly warm and inviting. Blessed and salubrious best encapsulated this space for living. I didn't want to leave, and also wanted to leave to inform others of this undercover beauty.

At the *heart* of Christianity there is *something* that enables it to be refused, misinterpreted, abused, deconstructed, and/or adopted by radically different cultures and people without being annihilated, but rather revitalized by this process. This because it is centered in and decentered by its "originating event, the regenerative centre that we call the resurrection."[1] This origin symbolized by the empty tomb is clearly given to sight as *Open: alive*, and is at the center of the Christian and Christianity, generating endless optimism. Our system of making meaning, of making a world that is meaningful, cannot access the interiority of phenomena nor overcome duality, but the Christian and Christianity are *sites* of something hidden that informs who we are and what we become. The Spirit of Christ claims to step into matter at a level, an interiority, that cannot be seen, and therefore does not dissolve particularity. This opens the Christian and Christianity to multiple possibilities, of releasing mystery through heterogenous articulations all of which perceptibly contain the *sacred*. The contamination of the *sacred* is inevitable given that it lives and loves at the mercy of the profaned. Sanctification[2] is a slow process of internal adjustment and mastery because of the fragility of human nature. One consequence of an infinite interiority is this: eschatology is not some future end point: apocalypse, as described in the book of Revelation. Apocalypse is already the Christian's and Christianity's condition interrupted. Resurrection is the internal state of Christians and Christianity as they continue to operate *as* and *through* sites of immanence. "Life itself" then "is essentially the *living* of something *other*; it is directed toward transcendence.[3]

The West is Christianized to the extent that Christianity has been internalized or interiorized, that is, it "underlies our existence" and "*all* our thinking is Christian through and through" as are many central institutions: the government, law, media, and rights that are foundational to democracy.[4] Should this estimation sound somewhat pious and totalizing, perhaps Jean-Luc Nancy's claim that "the modern world has evolved out of the Christian one" helps to reframe it.[5] If the West "is bound within the very fabric of Christianity" and at the heart of Christianity is a

1. Eastham, "Resurrection," 190.

2. Sanctification is a process of becoming more like Jesus (2 Cor 3:18).

3. Cain, *Gabriel Marcel*, 95.

4. Nancy, "Deconstruction of Christianity," 115.

5. Nancy, "Deconstruction of Christianity," 116.

"*transcendental absolute of opening up*" then, internal to the West is a radical capacity to "withstand almost anything that is thrown at it" and also "stretch to anything,"[6] provided that the West doesn't betray its very *heart*. Comparable to the Christian and Christianity, the Christianised West mirrors the outward bound movement of the Spirit despite the appropriative nature of its social contexts, situations and *milieu*. Limitless opportunities arise because at the *heart* of Christ, Christians, Christianity and Christianized West is essentially a victimized, resurrected, *open love* that is inappropriable, inexhaustible, and categorically with us. It stands to reason then, "Only through love can I [we, the West and Chrisitianity] gain access to the extreme limit of what is possible."[7]

Of increasing concern is the West's turning away from its Christian heart that generates a freedom in modernity responsible for abundance, and abundant tolerance. The words of Jesus ricochet like a bullet over eons and landscapes, cultures and people, never hitting its mark: "you can do nothing without me" (John 15:5). Integrity, and most notably the capacity to build and unify community in all of its eccentric difference, requires something stronger than politico-economic and cultural links. Talent, wealth, intellectual capital, property, and good works, indeed all human endeavour is of no value if the result is fracture, dissonance and the politics of indifference at the micro and macro levels. Despite increasing dysfunction, God says this: "*Australia is my ark!*"[8] Mirroring many Western democracies, the nature of the ark is corroborated through the extent of ethnic diversity and also in respect to its abundance, tolerance and benevolence, generally. We are safe from the flood, but for how long if we keep kicking against our spiritual pricks?

Bérulle believes with "our God given ability to select and desire comes the ability to resist the most powerful determinism. The

---

6. Nancy, "Deconstruction of Christianity," 114.

7. It is unclear the type of love being referred to here by Bataille, yet its salience is unequivocal. *Inner Experience*, 120.

8. This response was repeated three times.

ability is fragile and rarely employed but it opens a moral horizon."[9]
To him, selection and desire are potential implements of resistance.
In Augustine, "will" or "desire" indicates "that aspect of our being . . . which somehow has something and yet does not have it."[10]
Hannah Arendt, cited in Žižek's *On Belief*, suggests the possibility
that "an act of freedom is closer to the nature of miracle: freedom
is displayed in a capacity 'to begin something new and . . . not being able to control and even foretell its consequences.'"[11] Žižek adds
another dimension to the mix: "the truly free choice is a choice
in which I do not merely choose between two or more options
WITHIN a pre-given set of coordinates, but I choose to change
these coordinates as well . . . in the situation of a forced choice,
one ACTS AS IF THE CHOICE IS NOT FORCED and chooses
'the impossible.'"[12] A paradox has emerged: the desire to resist evil
is through human agency itself. Dominate evil with good,[13] is the
biblical dictum, but at what cost, one could ask? The incomparable
God-man of Nazareth now makes sense, and has the answer!

9. Domenach, "Voyage to the End," 155.

10. Milbank et al., *Radical Orthodoxy*, 10.

11. Žižek, *On Belief*, 113.

12. Žižek, *On Belief*, 121.

13. Rom 12:21.

Bibliography

Agamben, Georgio. *The Coming Community*. Translated by Michael Hardt. Minneapolis: The University of Minnesota Press, 1993.

———. "The Time That Is Left." *Epoché* 7.1 (2002) 1–14.

Bataille, Georges. *Inner Experience*. Translated and with an Introduction by Leslie Anne Boldt. Albany: State University of New York Press, 1988.

Brother Andrew. *God's Smuggler*. London: Hodder & Stoughton, 1967.

Brother Yun. *Living Water*. Edited by Paul Hattaway. Grand Rapids: Zondervan, 2008.

Boughton, Lynne C. "More Than Metaphors: Masculine-Gendered Names and the Knowability of God." *The Thomist* 58.2 (1994) 283–317.

Browning, Elizabeth Barrett. *Aurora Leigh and Other Poems*. London: Penguin, 1995.

Buber, Martin. *The Way of Response*. Edited by N. N. Glatzer. New York: Schocken, 1996.

Butler, Judith. *Bodies that Matter*. New York: Routledge, 1993.

Cain, Seymour. *Gabriel Marcel*. London: Bowes & Bowes, 1963.

Carter, Jimmy. *Sources of Strength*. New York: Three Rivers, 1997.

Collier, James F., dir. *The Hiding Place*. Executive produced by William F. Brown. Produced by Frank R, Jacobson. Worldwide Pictures Home Video, 1975.

Corretto, Carlo. *Letters From the Desert*. Foreword by Ivan Illich. London: Darton, Longman & Todd, 1972.

De Caussade, Jean-Pierre de. *Self-Abandonment to Divine Providence*. Translated by Algar Thorold. Introduction by David Knowles. Glasgow: Burns & Oates, 1959.

DeHaan, M. R., and H. G. Bosch. *Our Daily Bread*. Grand Rapids, MI: Zondervan, 1959.

Deleuze, Gilles. *Difference and Repetition*. Translated by Paul Patton. London: Athlone, 1994.

Derrida, Jacques. *The Gift of Death*. Translated by David Wills. Chicago: University of Chicago Press, 1995.

Bibliography

———. "Whom To Give To." In *Kierkegaard: A Critical Reader*, edited by Jonathan Rée and Jane Chamberlain, 151–74. Oxford: Blackwell, 1998.

Dickens, Charles. *A Tale of Two Cities*. Sydney, Australia: Amazon, 2020.

Domenach, Jean-Marie. "Voyage to the End of Man." In *Violence and Truth: On the Work of René Girard*, edited by Paul Dumouchel, translated by Mark A. Anspach, 152–59. London: Athlone, 1987.

Eastham, Scott. "Resurrection of the Word: The Origin of Christianity." *Colloquium* 32.2 (2000) 169–200.

Geisler, Norman L. "Chart of All the Supernatural Events Recorded in the Bible." *LifeCoach4God* (blog), June 18, 2013. https://lifecoach4god.life/2013/06/18/chart-of-all-the-supernatural-events-recorded-in-the-bible/.

Hamilton, Victor P. *The Book of Genesis, Chapters 18–50*. Grand Rapids, MI: Eerdmans, 1995.

Janzen, G. J. *Abraham and All the Families of the Earth: A Commentary on the Book of Genesis 12–50*. Grand Rapids, MI: Handset, 1993.

Kafka, Franz. *The Transformation and other Stories*. London: Penguin, 1992.

Kierkegaard, Søren. *Fear and Trembling*. Translated and introduction by Alastair Hannay. London: Penguin, 1985.

———. *Works of Love*. Translated by Bettina Bergo. Stanford: Stanford University Press, 1998.

Küng, Hans. *Eternal Life?* Translated by E. Quinn. London: Collins, 1984.

Lacugna, Cathrine Mowry. *God for Us: The Trinity and the Christian Life*. San Francisco: Harper, 1991.

Lien-Yueh Wei, Simon. "Dreams and Their Theological Meanings in Genesis." https://christ.org.tw/dream/dreams/dreams_in_genesis.htm.

Madsen, Catherine. "Notes on God's Violence." *Cross Currents* 51.2 (2001) 229–56.

———. "A Terrible Beauty: Moser's Bible." *Cross Currents* 50.1–2 (2000) 136–44.

Marion, Jean-Luc, *God Without Being*. Translated by Thomas A. Carlson. Chicago: Chicago University Press, 1991.

Milbank, John, et al., eds. *Radical Orthodoxy: A New Theology*. London: Routledge, 1999.

Mueller, George Friedrich. *The Autobiography of George Mueller*. Whitaker House: New Kensington, 1985.

Nancy, Jean-Luc. "The Deconstruction of Christianity." In *Religion & the Media*, edited by Hent de Vries and Weber Samuel, 113–30. Stanford, CA: California University Press, 2001.

———. *A Finite Thinking*. Edited by Simon Sparks. Stanford: Stanford University Press, 2003.

———. *The Inoperative Community*. Translated by Peter Connor et al. Edited by Peter Connor. Minneapolis: Minnesota University Press, 1991.

Nancy, Jean-Luc, et al. *Of the Sublime Offering: Presence in Question*. Translated by Jeffrey S. Librett. Albany: State University of New York Press, 1993.

Bibliography

Nietzsche, Fredrick. *The Gay Science*. Translated and with a commentary by Walter Kaufman. New York: Vintage, 1974.

Nouwen, Henri J. M. *The Genesee Diary: Report from a Trappist Monastery*, Garden City, NY: Doubleday, 1976.

Outka, Gene. *Agape: An Ethical Analysis*. New Haven: Yale University Press, 1972.

Saint Augustine. *The Confessions of St Augustine*. Translated by E. B. Pusey. London: Thomas Nelson, 1938.

Sobrino, Jon. *Christology at the Crossroads: A Latin American Approach*. Translated by John Druryl. London: SCM, 1978.

Steiner, George. "The Wound of Negativity: Two Kierkegaard Texts." In *Kierkegaard: A Critical Reader*, edited by Jonathan Rée and Jane Chamberlain, 103–13. Oxford: Blackwell, 1998.

St. John of the Cross. *Poems of St. John of the Cross*. Translated by Roy Campbell. Glasgow: Collins, 1951.

Taylor, Mark C. *Deconstructing Theology*. Edited by Thomas J. J. Altizer and James O. Duke. New York: Crossroad, 1982.

———. *Journeys to Selfhood*. Berkely: University of California Press, 1980.

Turner, Victor. *The Ritual Process: Structure and Anti-Structure*. Ithaca, NY: Cornell University Press, 1969.

Ward, Graham, ed. "Bodies: The Displaced Body of Jesus Christ." In *Radical Orthodoxy*, edited by John Milbank et al., 163–81. London: Routledge, 1999.

———. *The Postmodern God*. Malden: Blackwell, 1997.

———. "Transcorporeality: The Ontological Scandal." *The John Rylands Bulletin*, 1998.

Ward, Hannah. "Boundary Dwellers." *The Way* 33 (1993) 97–105.

Wurmbrand, Richard. *From Torture to Triumph*. Sussex: Monarch, 1991.

Žižek, Slavoj. *On Belief*. London: Routledge, 2001.

Zola, Émile. *Germinal*. Translated and with an introduction by L. W. Tancock. London Penguin,1954.